LOCAL RED BOOK

CHICHESTER BOGNOR REGIS

CONTENTS

Page Layout & Road Map 2
2½ Miles to 1 Inch

Chichester Enlarged Centre 3
8 Inches to 1 Mile

Street Maps
4 Inches to 1 Mi

Index to Str

Redbooks *showing the way*

Every effort has been made to verify the accuracy of information in this book but the publishers cannot accept responsibility for expense or loss caused by an error or omission.

Information that will be of assistance to the user of the maps will be welcomed.

The representation on these maps of a road, track or path is no evidence of the existence of a right of way.

Street plans prepared and published by ESTATE PUBLICATIONS, Bridewell House, TENTERDEN, KENT. The Publishers acknowledge the co-operation of the local authorities of towns represented in this atlas.

Ordnance Survey® This product includes mapping data licensed from Ordnance Survey® with the permission of the Controller of Her Majesty's Stationery Office.

071-15/08-03
ISBN 1 84192 297 8

www.ESTATE-PUBLICATIONS.co.uk

LEGEND

- Motorway
- 'A' Road
- 'B' Road
- Minor Road
- Pedestrianized / Restricted Access
- Track
- Built Up Area
- Footpath
- Stream
- River
- Canal (Lock)
- Railway / Station
- Post Office
- Car Park / Park & Ride (P, P+)
- Public Convenience (C)
- Place of Worship
- One-way Street
- Tourist Information Centre (i)
- Adjoining Pages (8, 8)
- Area Depicting Enlarged Centre
- Emergency Services
- Industrial Buildings
- Leisure Buildings
- Education Buildings
- Hotels etc.
- Retail Buildings
- General Buildings
- Woodland
- Orchard
- Recreational / Parkland
- Cemetery

Scale: 2½ Miles to 1 Inch

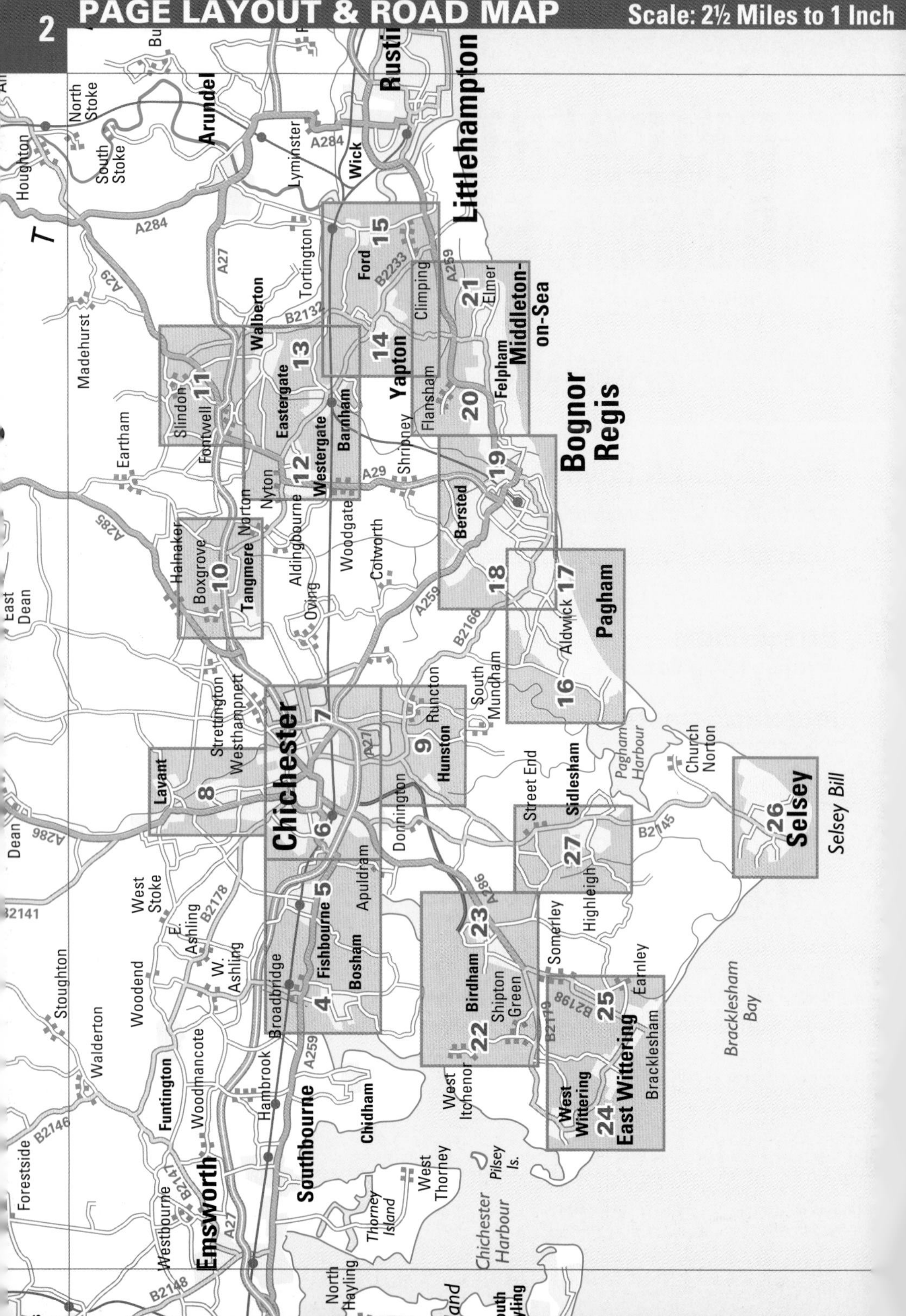

Arundel
North Stoke
South Stoke
Houghton
Lyminster
Wick
Littlehampton
A284
A27
A29
Madehurst
Walberton
Tortington
Ford
B2233
B2132
Climping
A259
Elmer
Middleton-on-Sea
Slindon
Fontwell
Eastergate
Yapton
Flansham
Felpham
Bognor Regis
Eartham
Westergate
Barnham
Shripney
Nyton
Norton
Aldingbourne
Woodgate
Colworth
Bersted
A285
Halnaker
Boxgrove
Tangmere
East Dean
Oving
B2166
Aldwick
Pagham
Strettington
Westhampnett
Chichester
Runcton
South Mundham
Lavant
Hunston
Donnington
Street End
Sidlesham
Pagham Harbour
Church Norton
Selsey
Selsey Bill
Dean
A286
Apuldram
B2145
Highleigh
West Stoke
B2178
E. Ashling
W. Ashling
B2141
Fishbourne
Bosham
Birdham
Somerley
Earnley
Stoughton
Woodend
Broadbridge
Shipton Green
B2179
B2198
East Wittering
Bracklesham
Bracklesham Bay
Walderton
Woodmancote
Funtington
Hambrook
A259
Southbourne
Chidham
West Itchenor
West Wittering
B2146
Forestside
Emsworth
B2147
Westbourne
Thorney Island
West Thorney
Pilsey Is.
Chichester Harbour
North Hayling
B2148
1 2 3 4 5 6 7 8 9 10 11 12 13 14 15 16 17 18 19 20 21 22 23 24 25 26 27

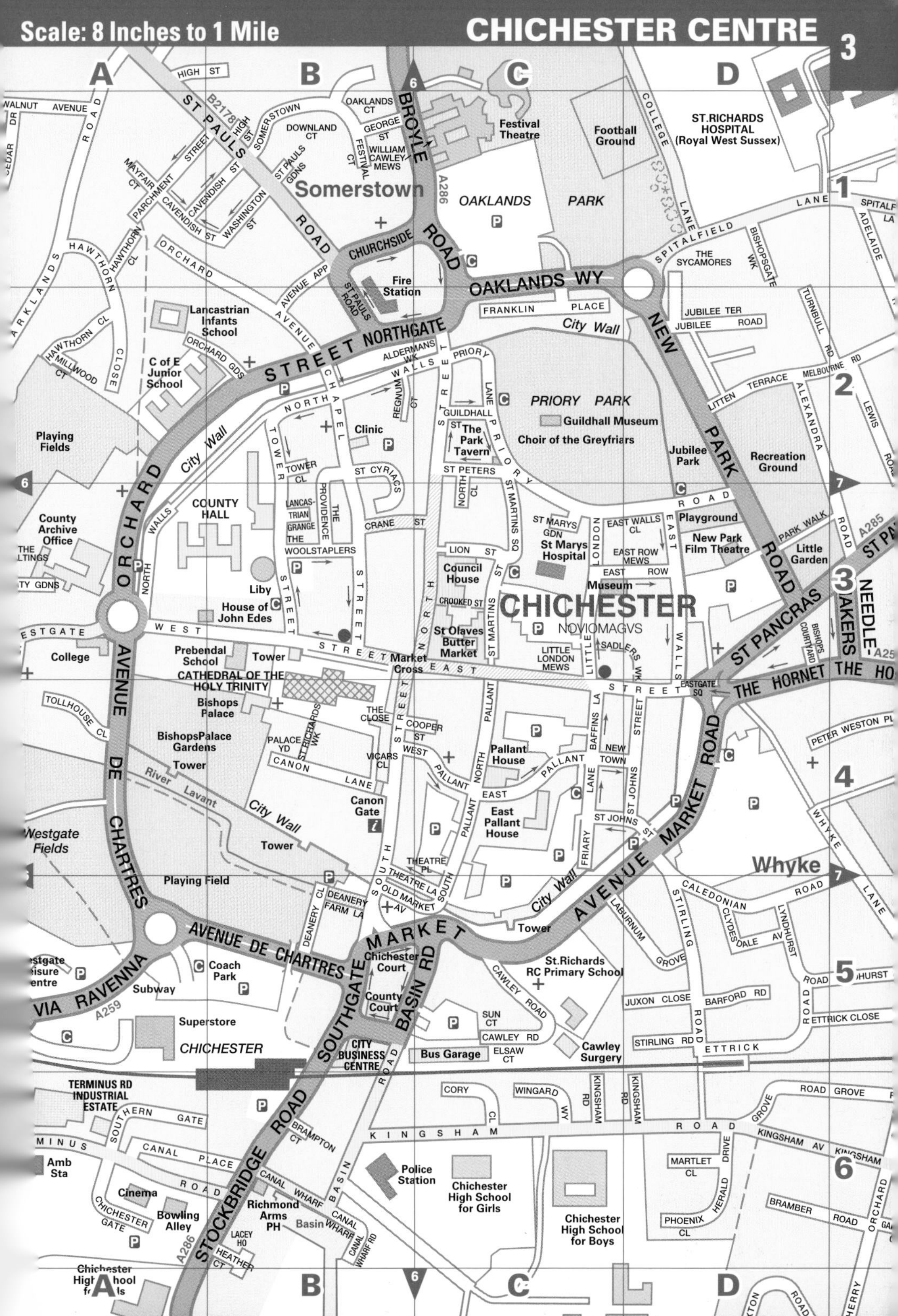
A
B
C
D
1
2
3
4
5
6
7
HIGH ST
WALNUT AVENUE
ST PAULS ROAD
B2178
SOMERSTOWN
DOWNLAND CT
OAKLANDS CT
GEORGE ST
WILLIAM CAWLEY MEWS
FESTIVAL CT
BROYLE ROAD
A286
Festival Theatre
Football Ground
COLLEGE LANE
ST.RICHARDS HOSPITAL (Royal West Sussex)
ST PAULS GDNS
Somerstown
MAYFAIR CT
PARCHMENT STREET
CAVENDISH ST
WASHINGTON ST
OAKLANDS PARK
SPITALFIELD LANE
HAWTHORN
HAWTHORN CL
ORCHARD
AVENUE APP
CHURCHSIDE
Fire Station
ST PAULS ROAD
OAKLANDS WY
THE SYCAMORES
BISHOPSGATE WK
ADELAIDE
FRANKLIN PLACE
JUBILEE TER
JUBILEE ROAD
TURNBULL RD
Lancastrian Infants School
ORCHARD GDS
C of E Junior School
HAWTHORN CL
MILLWOOD CT
CLOSE
ORCHARD AVENUE
STREET NORTHGATE
City Wall
ALDERMANS WK
PRIORY
NEW PARK ROAD
LITTEN TERRACE
MELBOURNE RD
ALEXANDRA
LEWIS
Playing Fields
NORTH WALLS
CHAPEL
REGNUM CT
Clinic
GUILDHALL
The Park Tavern
PRIORY PARK
Guildhall Museum
Choir of the Greyfriars
Jubilee Park
Recreation Ground
TOWER CL
ST CYRIACS
ST PETERS
NORTH CL
ST MARTINS SQ
County Archive Office
COUNTY HALL
LANCASTRIAN GRANGE
THE PROVIDENCE
CRANE ST
ST MARYS GDN
EAST WALLS CL
Playground
PARK WALK
A285
THE WOOLSTAPLERS
LION ST
St Marys Hospital
EAST ROW MEWS
New Park Film Theatre
Little Garden
Council House
EAST ROW
Museum
ST PANCRAS
NEEDLEMAKERS
Liby
House of John Edes
CROOKED ST
CHICHESTER
NOVIOMAGVS
WESTGATE
WEST STREET
St Olaves Butter Market
LITTLE LONDON MEWS
SADLERS WK
College
Prebendal School
Tower
Market Cross
EAST STREET
EASTGATE SQ
THE HORNET
CATHEDRAL OF THE HOLY TRINITY
Bishops Palace
TOLLHOUSE CL
THE CLOSE
COOPER ST
BAFFINS LA
PETER WESTON PL
BishopsPalace Gardens
PALACE YD
ST RICHARDS WK
NORTH PALLANT
NEW TOWN
Pallant House
WEST PALLANT
CANON LANE
VICARS CL
EAST PALLANT
MARKET ROAD
River Lavant
City Wall
Canon Gate
East Pallant House
ST JOHNS
ST JOHNS ST
WHYKE
Westgate Fields
SOUTH STREET
SOUTH PALLANT
FRIARY LANE
Whyke
THEATRE PL
THEATRE LA
OLD MARKET AV
Playing Field
DEANERY CL
DEANERY FARM LA
CALEDONIAN ROAD
CLYDESDALE AV
LYNDHURST
LABURNUM
STIRLING
AVENUE DE CHARTRES
Tower
MARKET AVENUE
GROVE
Westgate Leisure Centre
Coach Park
Chichester Court
St.Richards RC Primary School
Subway
County Court
CAWLEY ROAD
JUXON CLOSE
BARFORD RD
VIA RAVENNA
A259
SOUTHGATE
BASIN RD
SUN CT
ETTRICK CLOSE
Superstore
CHICHESTER
CITY BUSINESS CENTRE
CAWLEY RD
ELSAW CT
Bus Garage
Cawley Surgery
STIRLING RD
ETTRICK
TERMINUS RD INDUSTRIAL ESTATE
STOCKBRIDGE ROAD
CORY CL
WINGARD WY
KINGSHAM RD
ROAD GROVE
SOUTHERN GATE
BRAMPTON CT
KINGSHAM ROAD
KINGSHAM AV
TERMINUS
CANAL PLACE
Amb Sta
BASIN ROAD
Police Station
Chichester High School for Girls
MARTLET CL
HERALD DRIVE
ROAD
Cinema
CANAL WHARF
Chichester High School for Boys
BRAMBER ROAD
ORCHARD
CHICHESTER GATE
Bowling Alley
Richmond Arms PH
Basin
CANAL WHARF RD
PHOENIX CL
LACEY HO
HEATHER CT
Chichester High School for Girls

A
B
C
D
1
2
3
4
5
6
New Bar
Mudberry Farm
MUDBERRY LANE
NEWELLS LANE
Meadow Farm
GREEN LA
Bosham House
Colner House
A259
MAIN ROAD
Broad Bridge
Broadbridge Farm
LANE
B2146
Bosham Stream
The French Gardens (Nursery)
RATHAM
BOSHAM
Knapps Farm
BROOKS LANE
STANBURY CL
BROADBRIDGE MILL
HAMILTON GDNS
OLD BRIDGE RD
STATION RD
ARNOLD WAY
ROCKALL WY
WILLIAMS ROAD
BARNSIDE
Broadbridge
PENWARDEN WY
NORTH RD
GIFFORD RD
M'TONGUE AV
BROADBRIDGE DR
Ham Farm
Highgrove Farm
Colner Creek
Nursery
SOUTHFIELD INDUSTRIAL PARK
A259
ROAD
DELLING CL
Crede Farm
Walton Farm Nurseries
CHEQUER
Walton Farm
MARCUS FLDS
GREEN LA
Playing Field
ELM PK
CREDE CL
CREDE LANE
SCHOOL LA
School
Berkeley Arms PH
WINDMILL FIELD
CRITCHFIELD
Fire Station
WESTBROOK CL
WEST-BROOK
BROOK AV
DELLING LANE
WALTON LANE
MILES COTTAGES
WESTBROOK FIELD
THE HOLDENS
MERRY WEATHER RD
STREAM CL
MORETON RD
The Millstream Hotel
BOSHAM
SUNNY WAY
FAIRFIELD CL
FAIRFIELD RD
WESTWARD CL
ROAD
LEANDER RD
ASTRA
Rectory Farm
CHURCH MDW
Burial Grnd
CAMBRIA CL
HARBOUR CT
SHAMROCK CL
Moat
BOSHAM LANE
CANUTE RD
THE DRIVE
MANOR VILLAS
HARBOUR WY
Bosham
BOSHAM WK
HIGH ST
SHORE RD
MARINERS TER
SHORE
Jetty
HARBOUR RD
Hard
ROAD
STUMPS END
STUMPS LA
Bosham Quay
Channel
Stump's Farm
Churchfield Copse
Bosham
TAYLORS
PARK
OLD
SHORE
Southwood Farm
Petworth Cottage
LOWER HONE LA
Dunmere Pond

E   **F**   **G**   **H**

The Barracks

A27

CLAY

Stocker's
Copse

Salthill
House

Upper
Rouse
Copse

1

Polthooks
Farm

LANE

Hardham's
Farm

CLAY

SALTHILL

ROAD

A27

CHICHESTER

Salthill
Lodge

SALTHILL LA

SALTHILL

ORCHARD
COTTS

LANE

GODWIN
WY

HALFREY

STORRINGTON

VERICA
CT

FOLLIS
GDNS

SENATOR
GDNS

CLAY

2

Bethwines
Farm

BETHWINES
CL

HALFREY

HALFREY
ROAD

MOSSE

GDNS

Mead
House

NURSERY
LA

CLOSE

NEWPORT
DR

DEESIDE
AV

LANE

CLAY

6

BARKER

NEWPORT
DR

FREDERICK
RD

FISHBOURNE

BOURNE CL

Sch

WAY

FRE
ELAND

ALBERT
RD

WEST-
MEAD

Fishbourne

ROMAN
WW

GILPIN
CL

DOLPHIN
CL

P

Museum

WESTWARD
RD

CHRIS-
TOPHER

GROVE

3

MAIN

ROAD

MAIN

BLAKES
COTTS

SALTHILL
END

BEAVER
CL

CREEK

FISHBOURNE
ROMAN VILLA
(Remains)

FISHBOURNE
RD

EAST

WATERSMEET

FISHBOURNE

A259

ROAD

FISHBOURNE

BLACKBOY LANE

FARM

ROAD

BY-PASS

WEST

A27

APPLEDRAM

FERN
CL

Super

WEST

OLD

PARK

LANE

Leggatt's
Farm

Mill
Pond

MILL
LANE

MILL

CL

A259

The
Manor

APPLEDRAM LANE SOUTH

sery

4

6

Gothic
Farm

Old
Park

LANE

Manor
Farm

ewall
arm

PARK

Channel

Sewage
Works

APPLEDRAM LANE STH

5

APPLEDRAM LANE SOUTH

Chu
Far

Common
Farm

Fishbourne

6

Old Park
Farm

Apuldram
Manor
Farm

P

Rymans

APPLEDRAM

LANE

SOUTH

A28

Apuld

E   **F**   **G**   **H**

Dell

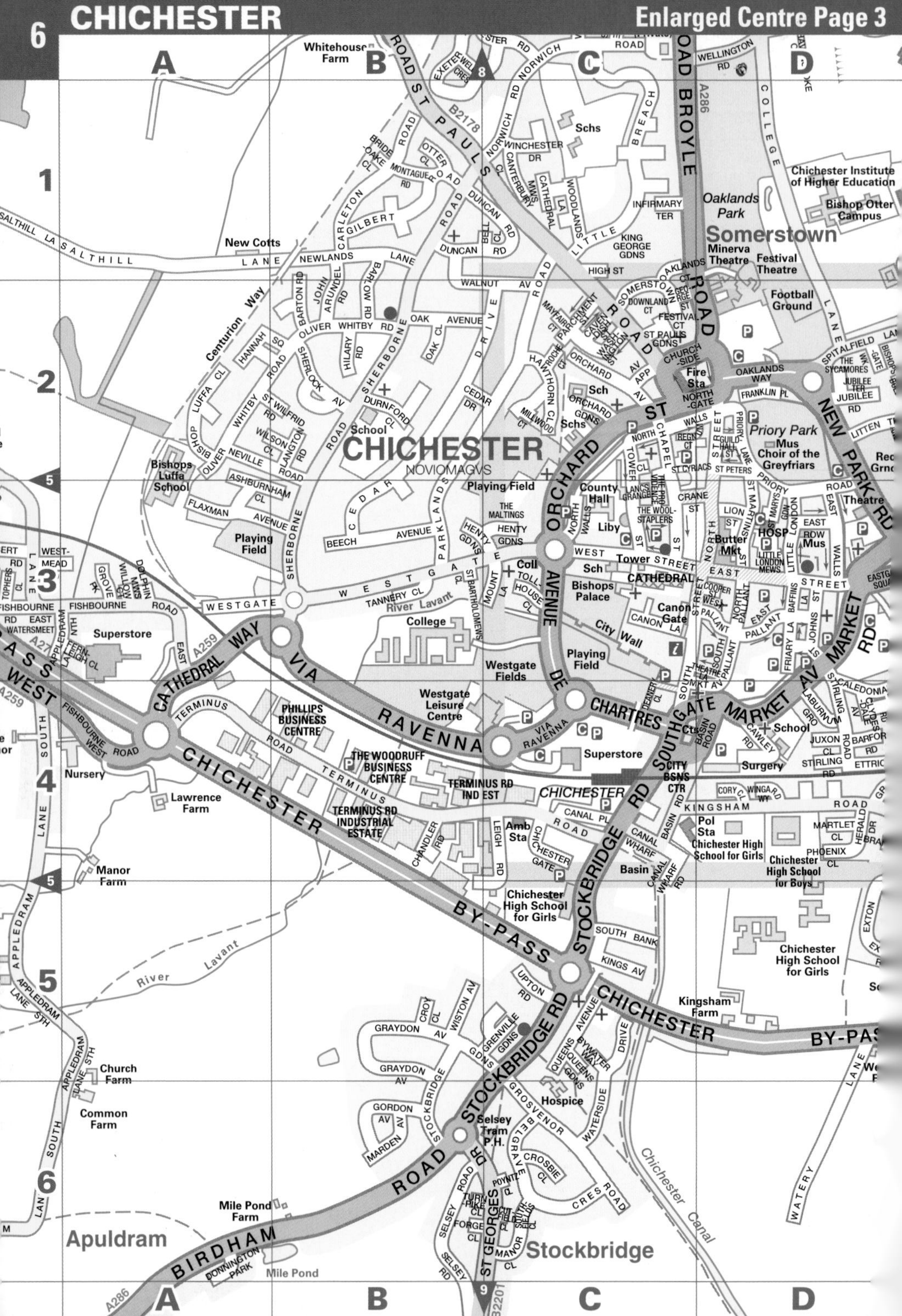
A
B
C
D
1
2
3
4
5
6
CHICHESTER
NOVIOMAGVS
Somerstown
Stockbridge
Apuldram
Whitehouse Farm
New Cotts
Oaklands Park
Minerva Theatre
Festival Theatre
Football Ground
Chichester Institute of Higher Education
Bishop Otter Campus
Priory Park
Mus
Choir of the Greyfriars
Theatre
HOSP
Butter Mkt
CATHEDRAL
Bishops Palace
Canon Gate
City Wall
County Hall
Liby
Coll
Sch
Schs
School
Bishops Luffa School
Playing Field
Superstore
College
Westgate Fields
Westgate Leisure Centre
PHILLIPS BUSINESS CENTRE
THE WOODRUFF BUSINESS CENTRE
TERMINUS RD IND EST
TERMINUS RD INDUSTRIAL ESTATE
CHICHESTER
CITY BSNS CTR
Amb Sta
Pol Sta
Chichester High School for Girls
Chichester High School for Boys
Basin
Surgery
Nursery
Lawrence Farm
Manor Farm
Church Farm
Common Farm
Mile Pond Farm
Mile Pond
Kingsham Farm
Hospice
Selsey Tram P.H.
Chichester Canal
River Lavant
Fire Sta
Cts
SALTHILL LA
SALTHILL LANE
NEWLANDS LANE
Centurion Way
CATHEDRAL WAY
VIA RAVENNA
CHICHESTER BY-PASS
FISHBOURNE WEST ROAD
WEST BY-PASS
STOCKBRIDGE RD
BIRDHAM ROAD
ST GEORGES DR
SELSEY ROAD
ORCHARD ST
AVENUE DE CHARTRES
SOUTHGATE
MARKET AV
MARKET RD
NEW PARK RD
BROYLE ROAD
ST PAULS ROAD
OAKLANDS WAY
WESTGATE
WEST STREET
EAST STREET
NORTH STREET
SOUTH STREET
TOWER STREET
SHERBORNE ROAD
PARKLANDS RD
CEDAR DR
OAK AVENUE
BEECH AVENUE
KINGSHAM ROAD
CANAL WHARF
APPLEDRAM LANE
APPLEDRAM LANE STH
APPLEDRAM LANE SOUTH
GRAYDON AV
GORDON AV
QUEENS AVENUE
WATERSIDE DRIVE
GROSVENOR RD
WATERY LANE
COLLEGE LANE
SPITALFIELD LANE
A27
A259
A286
B2178
B2201
8
9
5

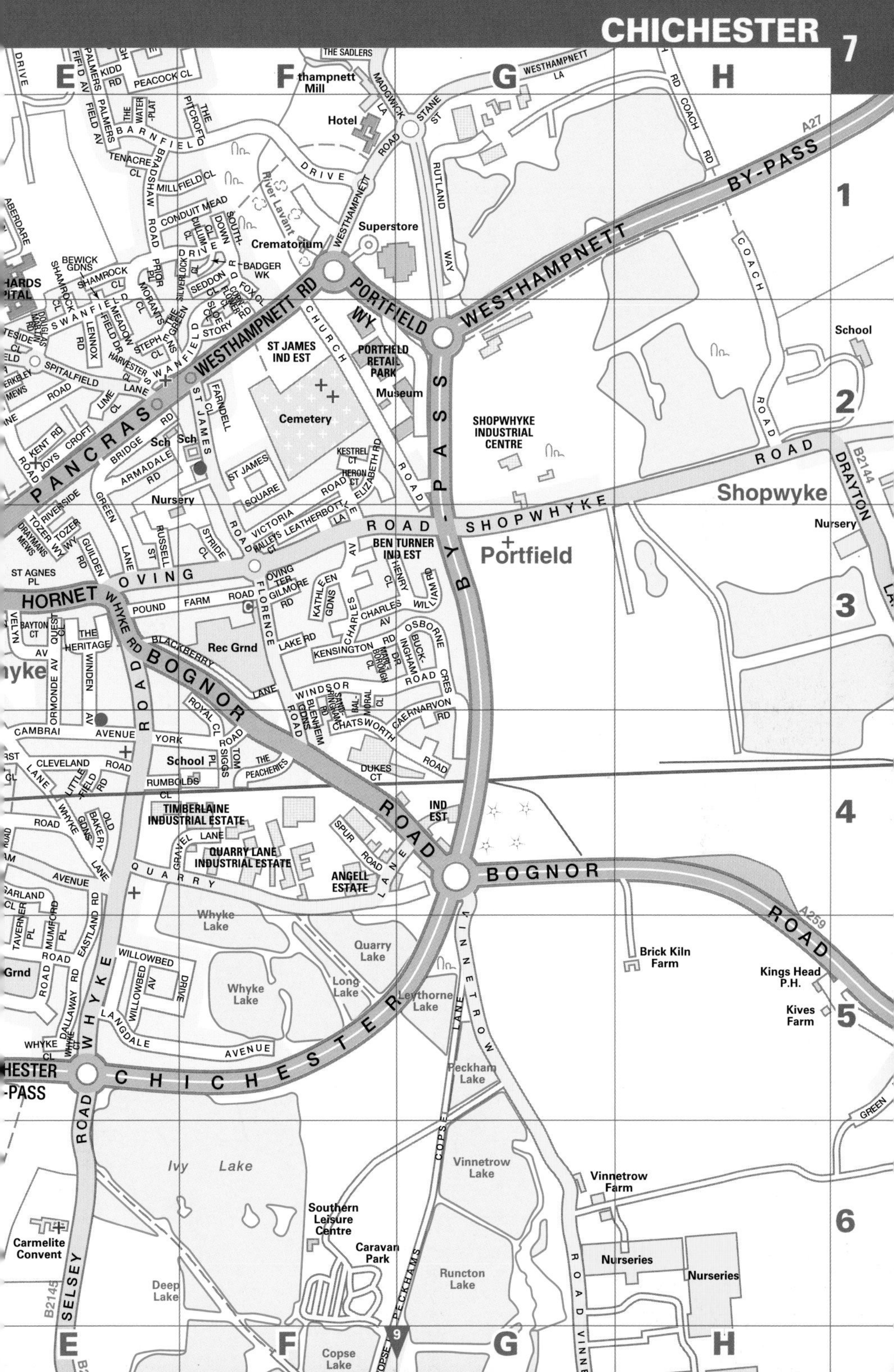
E
F
G
H
1
2
3
4
5
6
WESTHAMPNETT BY-PASS
A27
Westhampnett Mill
Hotel
Superstore
Crematorium
River Lavant
ST JAMES IND EST
PORTFIELD RETAIL PARK
Museum
Cemetery
SHOPWYKE INDUSTRIAL CENTRE
Shopwyke
Portfield
School
Nursery
SHOPWYKE ROAD
DRAYTON LA
B2144
BEN TURNER IND EST
PORTFIELD WY
BY-PASS
WESTHAMPNETT RD
ST PANCRAS
OVING ROAD
HORNET
Rec Grnd
BOGNOR ROAD
TIMBERLAINE INDUSTRIAL ESTATE
QUARRY LANE INDUSTRIAL ESTATE
ANGELL ESTATE
IND EST
School
Whyke Lake
Quarry Lake
Long Lake
Leythorne Lake
Peckham Lake
A259
Brick Kiln Farm
Kings Head P.H.
Kives Farm
CHICHESTER BY-PASS
Ivy Lake
Vinnetrow Lake
Vinnetrow Farm
Southern Leisure Centre
Caravan Park
Runcton Lake
Nurseries
Nurseries
Carmelite Convent
Deep Lake
Copse Lake
SELSEY ROAD
B2145
VINNETROW ROAD
COPSE LANE
PECKHAMS COPSE
9

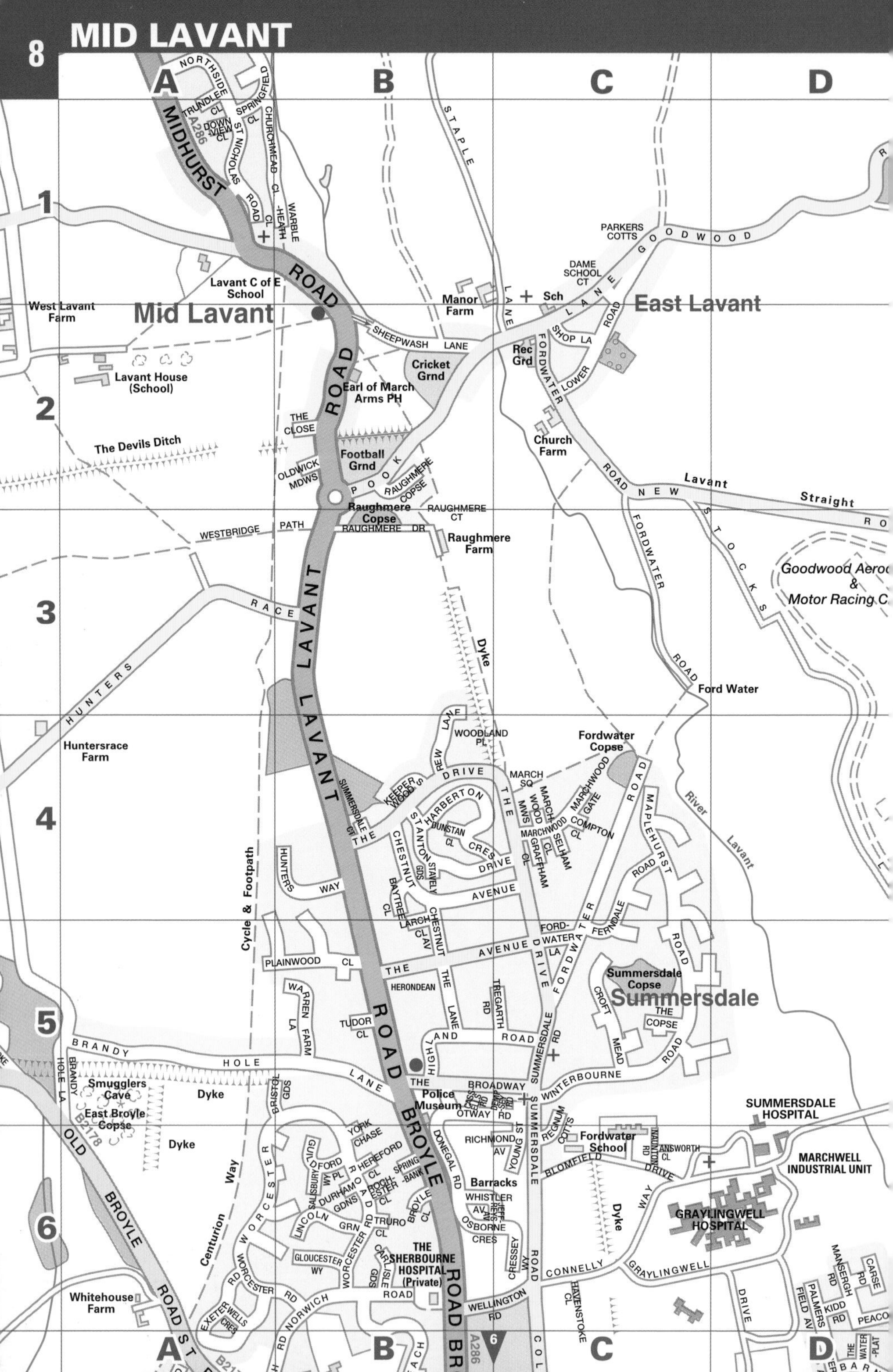
A
B
C
D
1
2
3
4
5
6
Mid Lavant
East Lavant
Summersdale
West Lavant Farm
Lavant House (School)
Lavant C of E School
The Devils Ditch
Manor Farm
Cricket Grnd
Earl of March Arms PH
Football Grnd
Raughmere Copse
Raughmere Farm
Rec Grd
Church Farm
Parkers Cotts
Dame School Ct
Sch
Goodwood Aero & Motor Racing C
Ford Water
Fordwater Copse
Huntersrace Farm
Cycle & Footpath
Centurion Way
Dyke
Smugglers Cave
East Broyle Copse
Summersdale Copse
Police Museum
Barracks
Fordwater School
Summersdale Hospital
Marchwell Industrial Unit
Graylingwell Hospital
The Sherbourne Hospital (Private)
Whitehouse Farm
River Lavant
Midhurst Road
Lavant Road
Broyle Road
Old Broyle Road
Sheepwash Lane
Staple Lane
Goodwood
Lavant Straight
New Road
Fordwater Road
Stocks Road
Hunters Race
Westbridge Path
Brandy Hole Lane
Summersdale Road
Highland Road
Winterbourne
Connelly
Graylingwell Drive
Wellington Rd
Norwich Road
Worcester Rd
A286
B2178
6

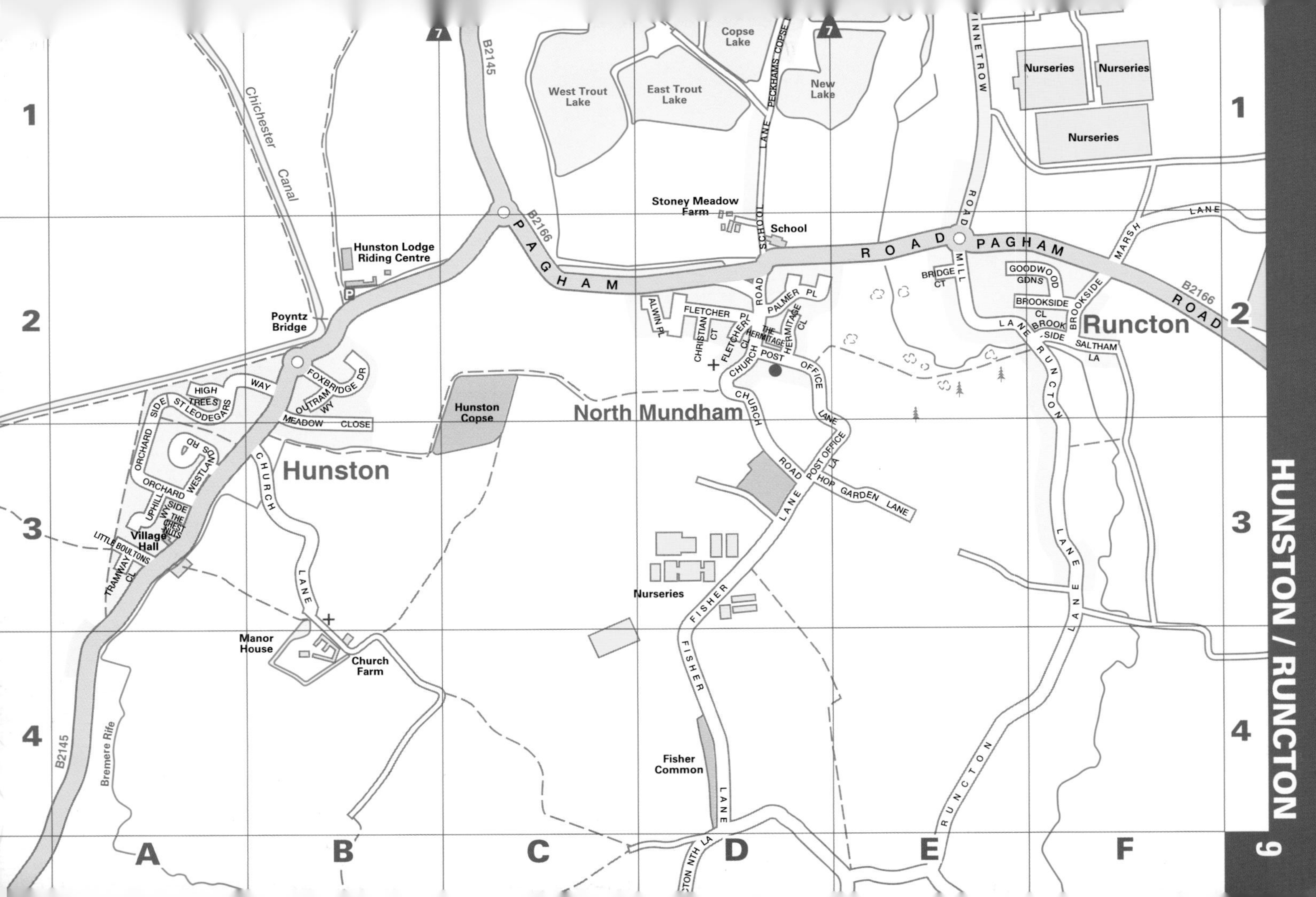
Runcton
North Mundham
Hunston
PAGHAM ROAD
B2166
B2145
RUNCTON LANE
MARSH LANE
BROOKSIDE
BROOKSIDE CL
BROOK SIDE
SALTHAM LA
GOODWOOD GDNS
BRIDGE CT
VINNETROW ROAD
MILL ROAD
SCHOOL LANE
PECKHAMS COPSE LANE
POST OFFICE LANE
POST OFFICE LA
HOP GARDEN LANE
CHURCH ROAD
CHURCH LANE
PALMER PL
HERMITAGE CL
THE HERMITAGE
FLETCHERS CL
FLETCHER PL
CHRISTIAN CT
ALWIN PL
FISHER LANE
RUNCTON NTH LA
Nurseries
New Lake
Copse Lake
East Trout Lake
West Trout Lake
School
Stoney Meadow Farm
Fisher Common
Hunston Copse
Hunston Lodge Riding Centre
Poyntz Bridge
Chichester Canal
FOXBRIDGE DR
OUTRAM WY
MEADOW CLOSE
MEADOW WAY
HIGH TREES
ST LEODEGARS
WESTLANDS RD
ORCHARD SIDE
ORCHARD
UPHILL WY
SIDE
THE CHESTNUTS
Village Hall
LITTLE BOULTONS
TRAMWAY CL
Manor House
Church Farm
Bremere Rife
A
B
C
D
E
F
1
2
3
4
7

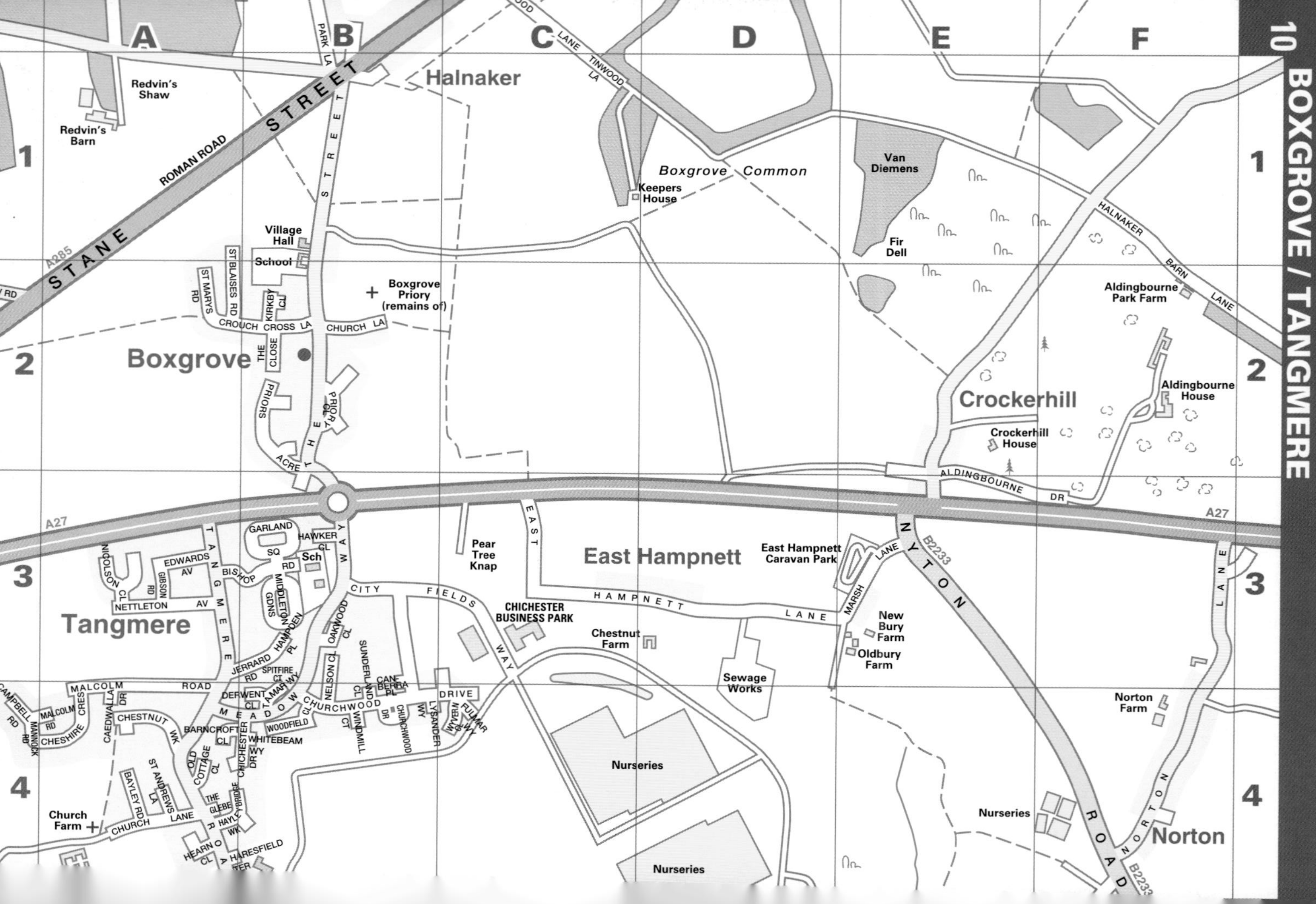

A B C D E F
1 2 3 4
Halnaker
Redvin's Shaw
Redvin's Barn
ROMAN ROAD
STANE STREET
A285
PARK LA
TINWOOD LANE
TINWOOD LA
Boxgrove Common
Keepers House
Van Diemens
Fir Dell
HALNAKER BARN LANE
Aldingbourne Park Farm
Aldingbourne House
Village Hall
School
Boxgrove Priory (remains of)
ST MARYS RD
ST BLAISES RD
KIRKBY CL
CROUCH CROSS LA
CHURCH LA
THE CLOSE
Boxgrove
PRIORS
PRIORY CL
THE ACRE
Crockerhill
Crockerhill House
ALDINGBOURNE DR
A27
GARLAND SQ
HAWKER CL
Sch
WAY
Pear Tree Knap
EAST HAMPNETT LANE
East Hampnett
East Hampnett Caravan Park
MARSH LANE
NYTON ROAD
B2233
LANE
NICOLSON CL
EDWARDS AV
GIBSON RD
TANGMERE ROAD
BISHOP RD
MIDDLETON GDNS
NETTLETON AV
CITY FIELDS WAY
CHICHESTER BUSINESS PARK
Chestnut Farm
New Bury Farm
Oldbury Farm
Sewage Works
Tangmere
HAMPDEN PL
OAKWOOD CL
SUNDERLAND CL
NELSON CL
CANBERRA PL
JERRARD RD
SPITFIRE CT
TAMAR WY
MALCOLM ROAD
DERWENT CL
MEADOW CL
CHURCHWOOD DR
DRIVE
LYSANDER WY
WYVERN CL
FULMAR WY
WINDMILL CT
CHURCHWOOD
CAMPBELL RD
MALCOLM RD
MANNOCK RD
CHESHIRE CRES
CAEDWALLA DR
CHESTNUT WK
BARNCROFT CL
WOODFIELD
WHITEBEAM WY
CHICHESTER DR
OLD COTTAGE CL
Norton Farm
Nurseries
BAYLEY RD
ST ANDREWS LA
THE GLEBE
HAYLEYBRIDGE WK
CHURCH LANE
Church Farm
HEARN CL
HARESFIELD TER
Norton
NORTON

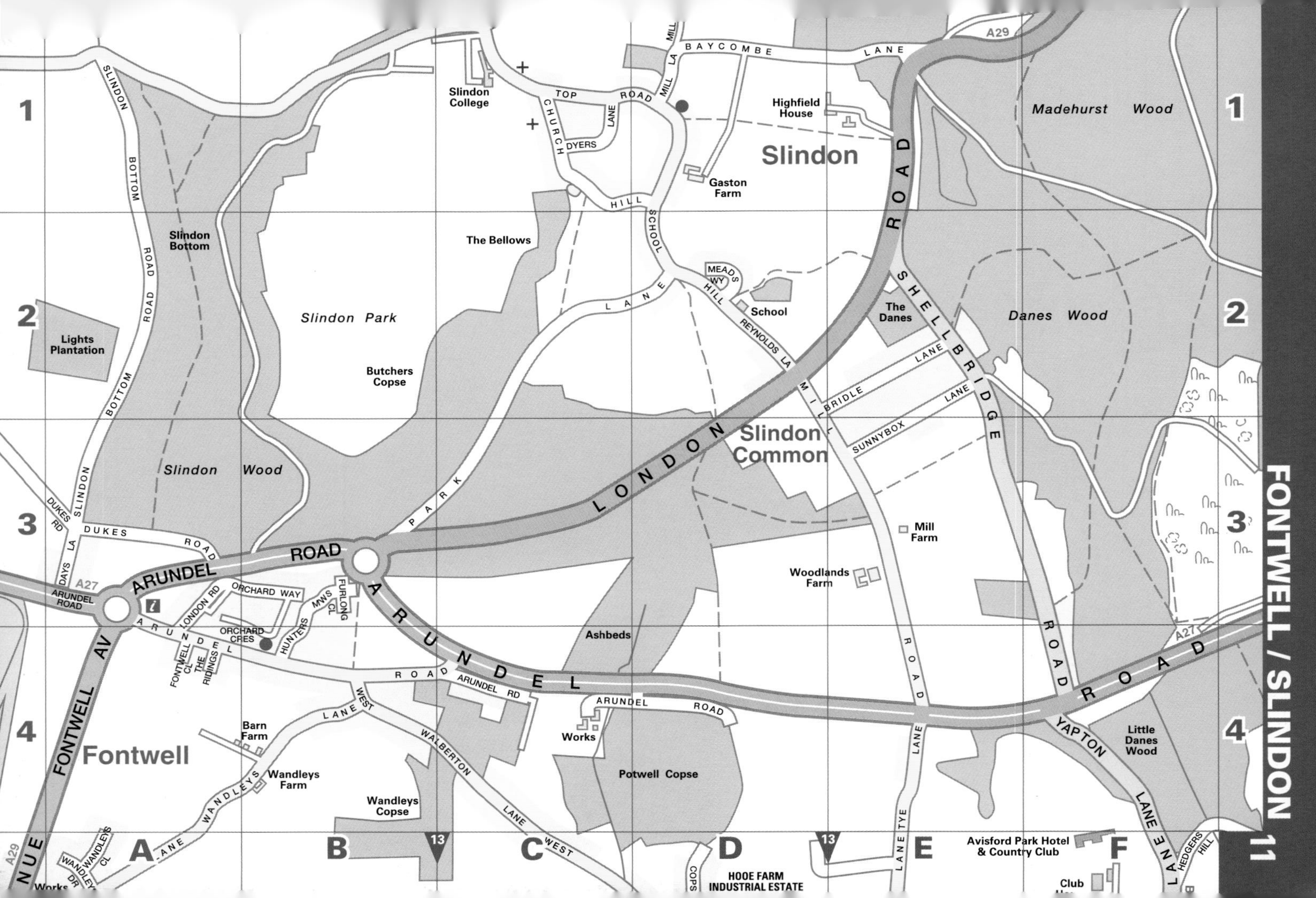

A29

1

2

3

4

HEDGERS HILL LANE

Madehurst Wood

Danes Wood

Little Danes Wood

YAPTON

LANE

F

Avisford Park Hotel & Country Club

Club

SHELLBRIDGE LANE

ROAD

The Danes

SUNNYBOX LANE

BRIDLE LANE

Mill Farm

ROAD

LANE

TYE LANE

E

ROAD

Slindon

Highfield House

Gaston Farm

School

REYNOLDS LA.

MEADS WAY

HILL

Slindon Common

Woodlands Farm

13

HODE FARM INDUSTRIAL ESTATE

D

COPS

LANE

BAYCOMBE

SCHOOL

LONDON

Ashbeds

ARUNDEL ROAD

Potwell Copse

Works

MILL LA.

MILL ROAD

TOP ROAD

LANE

HILL

DYERS

CHURCH

Slindon College

The Bellows

PARK

ARUNDEL

ROAD

WALBERTON LANE

WEST LANE

13

C

Wandleys Copse

B

Slindon Park

Butchers Copse

Slindon Wood

ROAD

ROAD

FURLONG CL.

MWS.

HUNTERS

WEST LANE

Wandleys Farm

Barn Farm

ORCHARD WAY

ORCHARD RD.

ORCHARD COPSE

LONDON RD.

THE RIDINGS

FONTWELL CL.

Slindon Bottom

ARUNDEL ROAD

ARUNDEL

A27

Fontwell

WANDLEYS LANE

Wandleys Farm

A

SLINDON BOTTOM ROAD

ROAD

BOTTOM

SLINDON BOTTOM

DUKES LA.

DAYS RD.

A27 ARUNDEL ROAD

FONTWELL AVENUE

WANDLEYS DR.

WANDLEY CL.

Lights Plantation

Works

A29

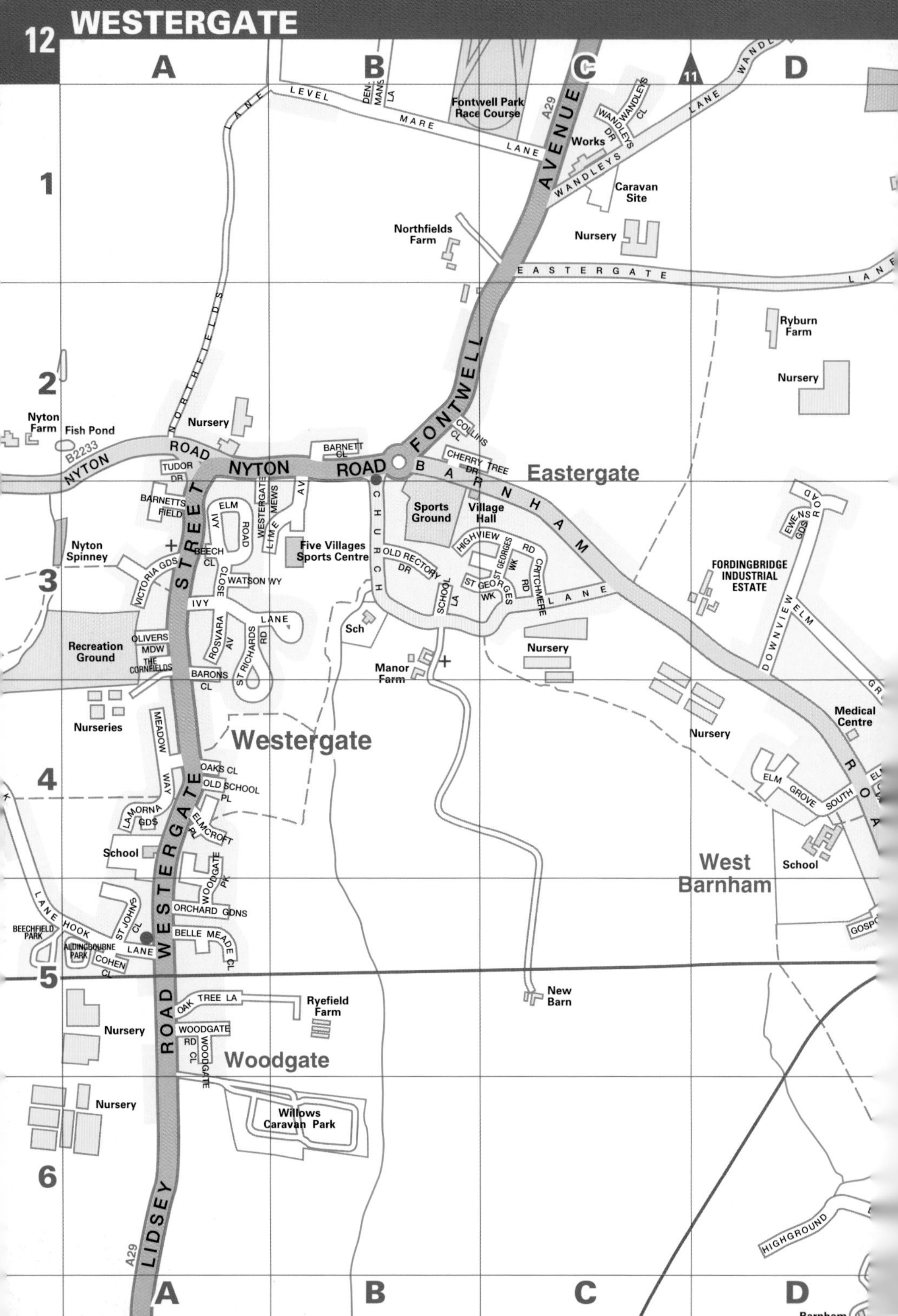

A B C A 11 D

1

LEVEL
LANE
DEN-MANS LA
MARE LANE
Fontwell Park Race Course
Works
WANDLEYS DR
WANDLEYS CL
WANDLEY
LANE
A29 AVENUE
Caravan Site

Northfields Farm

Nursery

EASTERGATE LANE

Ryburn Farm

Nursery

2

Nyton Farm
Fish Pond
B2233
NYTON ROAD
Nursery

NORTHFIELDS

FONTWELL

COLLINS CL
CHERRY TREE DR
BARNETT CL

Eastergate

Nursery

3

Nyton Spinney
TUDOR DR
BARNETTS FIELD
STREET
ELM ROAD
IVY
WESTERGATE MEWS
ELM
AV
Five Villages Sports Centre
BEECH CL
WATSON WY
VICTORIA GDS
Recreation Ground
OLIVERS MDW
THE CORNFIELDS
IVY
ROSVARA AV
ST RICHARDS RD
BARONS CL
LANE

CHURCH DR
OLD RECTORY DR
SCHOOL LA
Sch
Sports Ground
Village Hall
HIGHVIEW
ST GEORGES WK
ST GEORGES RD
CRITCHMERE
BARNHAM LANE
FONTWELL
ROAD

FORDINGBRIDGE INDUSTRIAL ESTATE
EWENS GDNS
ROAD
DOWNVIEW
ELM

Manor Farm
Nursery
Nursery
Medical Centre

4

Westergate

Nurseries
MEADOW WAY
LAMORNA GDS
School
OAKS CL
OLD SCHOOL PL
ELMCROFT PL
WOODGATE PK
ORCHARD GDNS
WESTERGATE

West Barnham

ELM GROVE SOUTH
School
ROAD

5

LANE
HOOK
BEECHFIELD PARK
ALDINGBOURNE PARK
ST JOHNS CL
COHEN CL
BELLE MEADE CL
LANE

New Barn

GOSPORT

6

Nursery
OAK TREE LA
WOODGATE RD CL
Ryefield Farm
Woodgate
WOODGATE

Nursery
Willows Caravan Park
A29
LIDSEY ROAD

HIGHGROUND
Barnham

A B C D

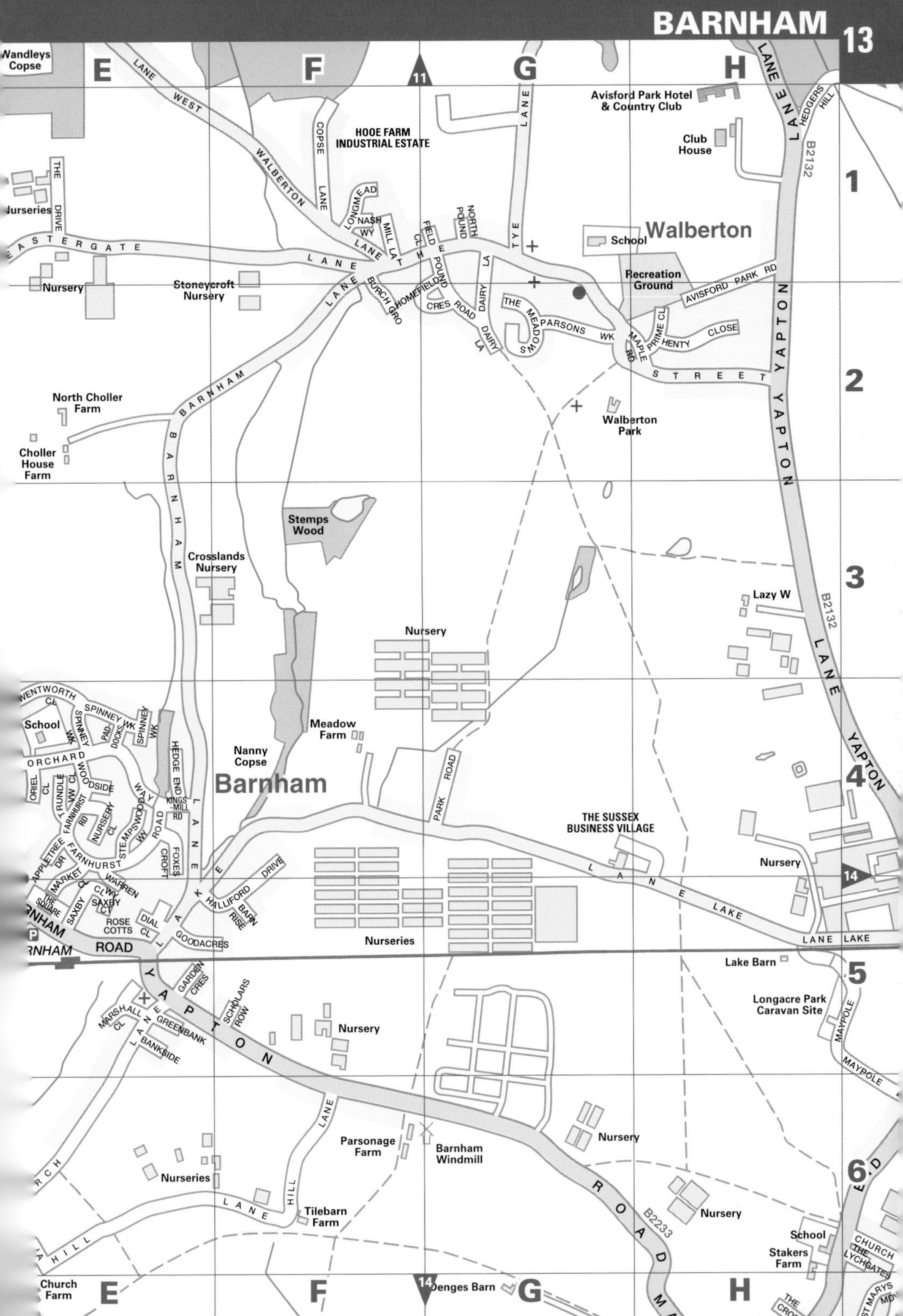

Wandleys Copse

E

F

11

G

H

LANE WEST

Avisford Park Hotel & Country Club

HOOE FARM INDUSTRIAL ESTATE

Club House

WALBERTON LANE

COPSE LANE

LANE

HEDGERS HILL

B2132

1

THE DRIVE

Nurseries

EASTERGATE

LONGMEAD

MILL LAT'H

NASH WY

FIELD CL

NORTH POUND

LANE

TYE

School

Walberton

Nursery

Stoneycroft Nursery

LANE

BURCH GRO

HOMEFIELD

POUND CRES

ROAD

DAIRY LA

THE MEADOWS

PARSONS WK

Recreation Ground

AVISFORD PARK RD

PRINE CL

HENTY CLOSE

YAPTON

BARNHAM

DAIRY LA

MAPLE RD

STREET

2

North Choller Farm

Walberton Park

Choller House Farm

YAPTON

BARNHAM

Stemps Wood

3

Lazy W

B2132

ROAD

Crosslands Nursery

Nursery

LANE YAPTON

WENTWORTH CL

School

SPINNEY WK

PAD'K DIOKS

SPINNEY WK

Meadow Farm

ORCHARD

ORIEL

FRUNDLE

FARNHURST

WOODSIDE

HEDGE END LANE

Nanny Copse

Barnham

PARK ROAD

4

Nursery

14

APPLETREE DR

FARNHURST CL

NURSERY

STEMPSWOOD WAY

KINGS MILL RD

FOXES CROFT

THE SUSSEX BUSINESS VILLAGE

LANE LAKE

Nursery

MARKET SQUARE

SAXBY CL

WARREN

CLWY

SAXBY CT

DIAL CL

HALLIFORD DRIVE

BARN RISE

LANE LAKE

Lake Barn

5

BARNHAM

ROSE COTTS

GOODACRES

ROAD

Nurseries

YAPTON

GARDEN CRES

GREENBANK

SCHOLARS ROW

Longacre Park Caravan Site

MAYPOLE

MAYPOLE

MARSHALL CL

BANKSIDE

Nursery

Nursery

LANE

THE CROFT

6

CHURCH HILL

Nurseries

LANE HILL

Parsonage Farm

Barnham Windmill

Nursery

ROAD MAIN

Nursery

School

Stakers Farm

CHURCH THE LYCHGATES

B2233

Church Farm

E

F

14

Denges Barn

G

H

ST MARYS MDW

D

13

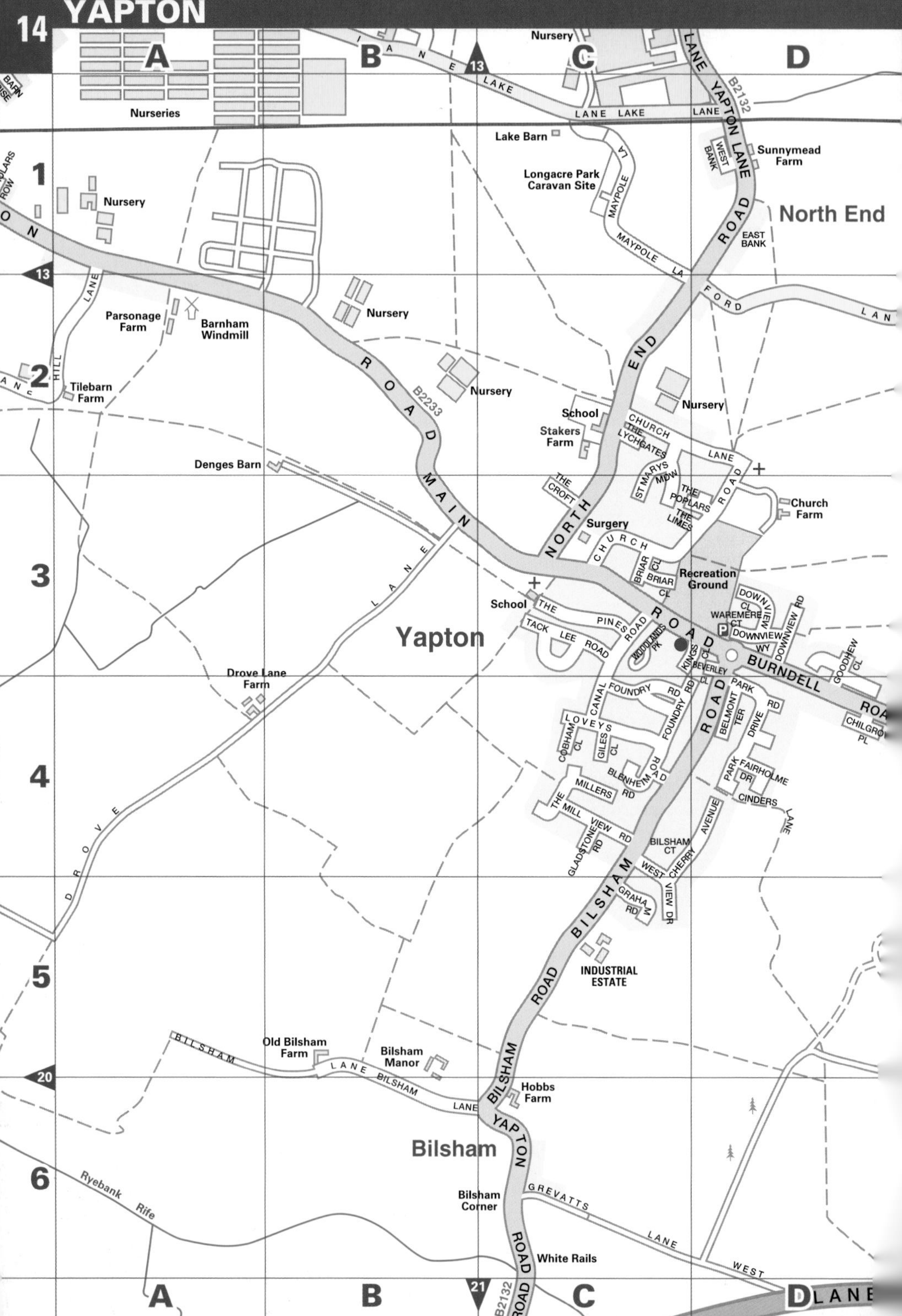

A   B   C   D

North End

Yapton

Bilsham

Nurseries

Nursery

Nursery

Parsonage Farm

Barnham Windmill

Tilebarn Farm

Denges Barn

Drove Lane Farm

Lake Barn

Longacre Park Caravan Site

Nursery

Nursery

School

Stakers Farm

THE CROFT

Surgery

School

TACK LEE ROAD

THE PINES

WOODLANDS PK

KINGS CL

Recreation Ground

Sunnymead Farm

WEST BANK

EAST BANK

CHURCH THE LYCHGATES

ST MARYS

MDW

THE POPLARS

THE LIMES

Church Farm

BRIAR CL

BRIAR CL

WAREMERE

DOWNVIEW CT

DOWNVIEW RD

DOWNVIEW WY

BEVERLEY CL

BURNDELL

GOODVIEW CL

CHILGROVE PL

ROAD

LOVEYS CL

GILES CL

FOUNDRY RD

FOUNDRY RD

BLENHEIM RD

PARK DRIVE

BELMONT TER

PARK

FAIRHOLME DR

CINDERS

THE MILL

MILLERS RD

GLADSTONE RD

MILL VIEW RD

BILSHAM CT

WEST CHERRY VIEW DR

GRAHAM RD

AVENUE

LANE

BILSHAM ROAD

INDUSTRIAL ESTATE

BILSHAM

Old Bilsham Farm

Bilsham Manor

Hobbs Farm

Bilsham Corner

White Rails

Ryebank Rife

GREVATTS LANE

WEST

YAPTON ROAD

B2132

DROVE LANE

ROAD MAIN

NORTH END ROAD

MAYPOLE LA

YAPTON LANE

B2132

LANE LAKE LANE

Nursery

FORD LANE

13

20

21

A   B   C   D

E   F   G   H

1

2

3

4

5

6

GAUDEMASTER WY THE WILLOWS

FORD

Arundel Arms P.H.

STATION ROAD

Caravan Park

Long Barn

FORD

Wicks Farm

TRADING ESTATE

Marina

River Arun

Lower Farm

LANE

FORD

Ford

RODNEY CRES

Works

NELSON ROW

FORD AIRFIELD INDUSTRIAL ESTATE

JOHNSON

FORDWATER GDNS

MUSTANG CL

LEWIS LA

BEAGLE

DR WILSON

WILLS

PARK

SPROULE

YAPTON

DRAKE

JUNCTION GRO

DOUGLAS CL

MILES

WAY

ROLLASTON

HM PRISON FORD

HM PRISON FORD

Ford Airfield (disused)

ARNDELL RD

RD

ROAD YAPTON

ROAD YAPTON RD

RUDFORD INDUSTRIAL ESTATE

Church Farm

ROAD

CHURCH LANE

Climping

GREEN

HORSEMERE

APPLE TREE WK

CROPTHORNE DR

LANE

Caravan Park

YAPTON

Northwood Farm

Horsemere Green

B2233 ROAD

LANE GREVATTS LA CROOKTHORN

A259

CROOKTHORN LANE

A259 LANE

School

Kent's Farm

Hobbs Farm

CLIMPING STREET

LANGMEADS CL

CLIMPING

GREVAT

21

E   F   G   H

A B C D

1

2

3

Nyetimber

4

5

Pagham

6

A B C D

North Honer Farm

Bowley Farm

Sefter Farm

Sefter Bottom

Pagham Rife

Sewage Works

Furzefield Barn

Oak Tree Cl

Mill Farm, Park Home Estate

Rookery Farm

Rose Grn
Rossalyn Cl
Rose Green Cnty Primar School

Rose Green Cnty Primary School
& Youth Centre

Bear Inn
Pol Sta
The Lion
Nyetimber
Cricket Grnd
Sylvia Cl
Liby
Lamb Inn
Church Barton House

Shipverling Barn

Aldwick Bay Estate

Tithe Barn Club

Little Welbourne

Church Farm Club

Church Farm Holiday Village

Becket's Barn

Kings Beach Hotel
Clinic
Mulberry Ct
Churchill Ct

Pagham Lagoon

Rose Green

Avisford Park

Copthorne Caravan Site

Aldwick

The Martlets PH

School

West Park

The Ship PH

Craigweil on Sea

Barn Rock Estate

Craigweil Manor

Gate

Aldwick

Barn Rocks

CHANNEL

ENGLISH

North Bersted
Orchard Caravan Site
Morells Farm
Copthorne Caravan Site
The Royal Oak PH
Stamps PH
Bartons Inf Sch
Playing Field
Community Centre
Chalcroft Nursery
Cemetery
Newtown Social Club
The Michael Ayres County Junior School
Bognor Regis Comm Coll
The Arena
The Glade Infants School
Howard House
Rec Grnd
Fire Sta
Bognor Regis School
School
Cricket Ground
Football Ground
Courts
The Martlets PH
The Ship PH
West Park
CHICHESTER ROAD
LOWER BOGNOR ROAD
ALDWICK ROAD
ALDWICK RD
CHALCRAFT LANE
HAWTHORN ROAD
NEWTOWN AVENUE
CENTRAL AVENUE
NORTH BERSTED STREET
ROWAN WAY
WESTMINSTER DRIVE
FISH LANE
MARINE DRIVE WEST
A259
B2166

E
F
G
H
1
2
3
4
5
6
Aldingbourne Rife
Caravan Club Site
Oldlands Farm
Retail Centre
Riverside Caravan Park
Poplars Caravan Park
SOUTHERN CROSS INDUSTRIAL ESTATE
ASH GROVE INDUSTRIAL PARK
CLOCK PARK
ARUN RETAIL PARK
SOUTH BERSTED INDUSTRIAL ESTATE
Supermarket
ARUN BUSINESS PARK
SHRIPNEY ROAD
School
Sch
HOSPITAL
Community College
Arun Leisure Centre
Recreation Ground
Playing Field
Hotham Park
Edward Bryant County Primary School
Bognor College Education
BUTLINS SOUTHCOAST WORLD
Longbrook Park
Cinema
Health Centre
Mus
Town Hall
Theatre & Bognor Regis Centre
Pier Theatre
BOGNOR REGIS
UPPER BOGNOR RD
FELPHAM WAY
HOTHAM WAY
CHICHESTER ROAD
PROMENADE
ESPLANADE
Lidsey Rife
Golf
Club House
20

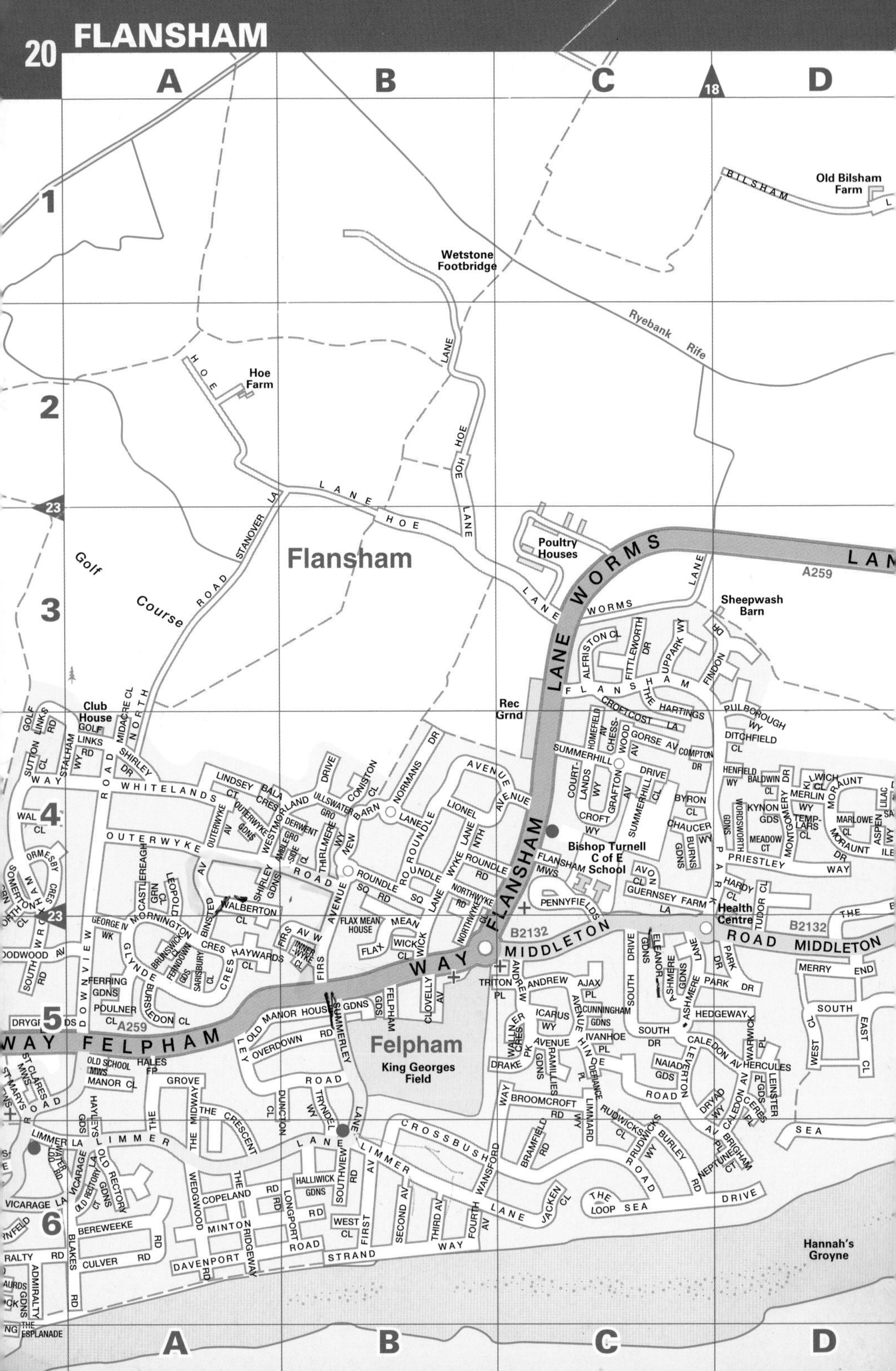
A
B
C
D
18
1
2
3
4
5
6
23
Old Bilsham Farm
BILSHAM
Wetstone Footbridge
Ryebank Rife
Hoe Farm
HOE LANE
Flansham
Golf Course
STANOVER LA
NORTH ROAD
Poultry Houses
WORMS LANE
A259
Sheepwash Barn
Club House
Rec Grnd
FLANSHAM LANE
FLANSHAM
Bishop Turnell C of E School
Health Centre
B2132
MIDDLETON ROAD
FELPHAM WAY
Felpham
King Georges Field
SEA DRIVE
THE LOOP
Hannah's Groyne
THE ESPLANADE
A
B
C
D

Bilsham

Middleton-on-Sea

INDUSTRIAL ESTATE

Bilsham Manor

Hobbs Farm

Bilsham Corner

White Rails

Guernsey Farm

MIDDLETON BUSINESS PARK

Ancton

St Nicholas

Rec Grnd

Sports Ground

Elmer

Lane End Farm Caravan Site

Grevatts Bridge

Hobb's New Barn

Northwood Farm

Ryebank Rife

Poole Place

Site of Medieval Village of Middleton

BILSHAM ROAD

YAPTON ROAD

GREVATTS LANE

WEST LANE

LANE GREVATTS

A259

LANE GREVA

WORMS LA

B2132

B2132

YAPTON ROAD

ANCTON ROAD

CHURCH PATH

LANE

KINGSMEAD GDS

KINGSMEAD

SUNNYMEAD

ANCTON

ANCTON DRIVE

LANE

ROAD CENTRAL

ELM DRIVE

SEA WAY

WAY

STABLE FIELD

E F G H

A   **B**   **C**   **D**

SMUGGLERS LANE

HOE LA

Boat Yard

Furzefield Creek

Jetties

1

Bosham Hoe

Upper Wolves Copse

Passenger Ferry (Seasonal)

Chichester

Jetty

Lower Wolves Copse

2

STREET

CHANDLERS REACH

Jetties

Jetties

Long Pe

Itchenor Park

P

West Itchenor

THE ROAD

ORCHARD LA

WATERSTONE CL

Channel

Jetties

Jetty

3

Itchenor House

ITCHENOR ROAD

SPINNEY

LANE

Westlands Copse

Westlands Farm

WESTLANDS LA

GR

4

THE SPINNEY

CHALKDOCK LA

5

GLEBE FIELD RD

ITCHENOR ROAD

Shipton Green

Caravan Park

Lippering Farm

Redlands Moat

SHEEPWASH LANE

REDLANDS LANE

SHIPTON

GREEN LANE

ROA

6

Wicks Farm Caravan Park

PEL LA

CHAPEL LA

FERRY HALF LA

ITCHENOR LA

CHICHESTER ROAD

Hot Place

Guys Farm

Northleigh Farm

179

A   **B**   ▽25   **C**   **D**

E **F** **G** **H**

Trews Copse

Oldpark Wood

Copperas Point

New Barn

1

Chichester Channel

...etcher's Copse

Salterns Copse

2

Chichester

Marina

Salterns Lock

Birdham Pool

Marina

Shipyard

Egremont Swing Bridge

Chichester Canal

P

Westlands Pier

HARBOUR MDW

THE CAUSEWAY

LOCK LANE

LOCK LA

3

A286

ROAD

...ACRES

WESTLANDS

COURT

BARN LANE

OAK MEADOW

Birdham

Birdham Fruit Farm

Broomer Farm

CHURCH LANE

MARTINS LANE

ALLMAN BUSINESS PARK

...STLANDS

LANE

ST JAMES CL

KEWELLS GDNS

CLAYTONS DRI

CHURCH RD

Cowdray Farm

4

PESCOTTS CL

CHERRY LA

SPRINGFIELD CL

SIDLESHAM ROAD

School

THE SALTINGS

FLORENCE CL

LONGMEADOW GDNS

WALWYN CL

ALANDALE ROAD

5

CHAFFER LA

FLORENCE LA

CROOKED

M A I N

FARNE LA

FARNE LA

Nurseries

27

BURLOW CL

OLD SCHOOL CL

Whitestone Farm

Woodhorn Farm

6

...rsery

BELL LANE

PINKS LANE

LANE

BATCHMERE RD

MAPSONS LANE

JOCK... G

E **F** **G** **H**

A
B
C
D
1
2
3
4
5
6
Nunnington Farm
Nunnington Farm Caravan Park
Playing Field
B2179
ROAD
ROMAN LANDING
ROMAN LANDING
SUMMERFIELD ROAD
CUNLIFFE CL
LOCKSASH CL
ROOKWOOD
ELMSTEAD PARK RD
ELMS WAY
MEADOW LA
ELMS LANE
ELLANORE LANE
POUND RD
Snow Hill
West Wittering Primary School
COASTGUARD LANE
CAKEHAM
ROYCE CL
ROYCE WAY
ELMS RIDE
Home Farm
WAD
THE WAD
MIDFIELD CL
HOLMWOOD
SEAWARD DR
THE BYEWAY
WELLSFIELD
West Wittering
BERRYBARN LANE
WEST STRAND
EAST STRAND
Cakeham Manor House
ROAD
CAKEHAM ROAD
B2179
Webb's Farm
Scotts Farm Caravan Park
RUSSELL ROAD
AVENUE ROAD
HOWARD AVENUE
SUNNINGDALE GDNS
SOUTHCOTE AV
ELLA CL
CULIMORE CL
CULIMORE RD
THE CRES
Health Ce
MARINE DRIVE WEST
WEST BEACH ROAD
JOLLIFFE
OWERS WY
MARINE DRIVE
WEST BEACH
MARINE DRIVE
CLOSE
WATERSIDE GDNS
SEAGATE CT
SHORE
BRACKLESHAM BAY

E   **F**   **G**   **H**

Holmes Farm

ACRE STREET

CHAPEL LANE

PIGGERY

HUNDREDSTEDDLE LA

Hundredstedle Farm

1

Nurseries

HALL

Somerley

B2198

BELL LANE

SOMERLE LA

Tile Barn Estate

LANE

TILE BARN LA

LANE

2

Briar Cottage Caravan Park

FURZEFIELD

BRIAR AV

PIGGERY

Glen Nurseries

LANE

Thatched Tavern PH

CHURCH RD

FARM

Museum

Caravan Park

Residential Home

CHURCH

HILTON

PARK

STUBCROFT LANE

BOOKERS

EAST WITTERING BUSINESS CENTRE

3

ROAD

Stubcroft Farm

LANE

Cherry Tree Farm

BOOKERS

East Wittering

CHAUCER DR

BENNETTS

CL

MILL

CLAYTON LA

BRACKLESHAM

LANE

EARNLEY RD

ROAD

Police Ho

Youth Centre

TOWER PL

ST ANNES

CHURCH

HAVEN CT

ROAD

B2198

Holdens Farm Caravan Park

LANE

EARNLEY

4

School

BARN

RFIELDS RD

MEADOWS RD

WESSEX AV

STUBCROFT

BRACKLESHAM

South Downs Holiday Park

BOOKERS LANE

EARNLEY MANOR CL

OAKFIELD

STOCKS

SOUTHDOWN CT

DOWNVIEW CL

CLAPPERS

DROVE

SOLENT

AVENUE

ROAD

CONEY

SEAFIELD CL

BARTON WY

Earnley

Adult Education Centre

5

NAB WK

SHINGLE ROAD

CONEY SIX

CONEY SIX

CHARLMEAD

CHARLMEAD

SEAFIELD WY

PEERLEY NAGELS

KIMBRIDGE CL

MIDDLETON

HALE

GRAYS AV

GARDEN AV

CLOSE

ELM

BEECH

LANE

DROVE

WEST

BRACKLESHAM

PEERLEY CL

LEGION CL

ROAD

SAND PIPER CT

CORMORANT CT

KESTREL CT

PLOVER CT

WAY

BRACKLESHAM

BRACKLESHAM CT

CROSTOCK CT

POND

BEECH AV

Bracklesham

SANDRINGHAM DR

HARMONY

ELCOMBE CL

WOOD

BOROUGH

CL

6

BOURNE CT

DRIVE

LANE

EAST FARM

OLD FARM

FIRST AV

SECOND AV

ROAD

THIRD AV

WILTON CL

SHALBOURNE CL

SAVEBURY CL

MAWTON CL

CRESCENT

GPO

Bracklesham Bay

BRACKLESHAM

MARINESIDE

SEAFIELDS

SUSSEX WY

WALMSLEYS WY

SILVER WY

DRIVE

LEIGH

Bracklesham Bay Caravan & Boot Club

E   **F**   **G**   **H**

Grid references: 1, 2, 3, 4 (top and bottom), A, B, C, D, E, F (sides)

Major features:
- East Beach
- English Channel
- Selsey Bill
- Selsey
- Lifeboat Station
- Lifeboat Museum
- Coastguard Station

Roads and streets (selection):
- EAST BEACH ROAD
- PARK LANE
- NEWFIELD ROAD
- GILLWAY
- CHICHESTER ROAD
- THE CLOSE
- FONTWELL WAY
- BEACH WAY
- ORCHARD PARADE
- COASTABLE LANE
- PARK DRIVE EAST
- EAST DRIVE
- NORTHFIELD
- RUSKIN
- BEVERLEY
- FRASER
- MERRYFIELD
- BURLINGTON GDNS
- MARINE DRIVE
- BROAD VIEW
- ALBION STREET
- SUNNYSIDE
- BEACON
- JAMES STREET
- LAWRENCE ROAD
- THE LIFEBOAT PH
- WARNER ROAD
- HILLFIELD ROAD
- CLAYTON
- VINCENT ROAD
- MURRAY RD
- BONNAR
- SEAL ROAD
- SEAVIEW
- DRIFT LANE
- CRABLANDS
- HIGH STREET
- EAST STREET
- SCHOOL LANE
- CHURCH
- ST PETERS
- MANOR ROAD
- GOLF LINKS LANE
- UPWAYS
- B2145
- BEACH ROAD

Caravan parks and sites:
- Green Lawns Caravan Site
- White Horse Caravan Park
- West Mount Caravan Park
- The Nook Caravan Park
- Goathlands Caravan Park
- West Sands Caravan Park
- Warners Farm
- Mill House

Other points of interest:
- Pol Sta (Police Station)
- Playing Field
- Football Ground
- Fire Sta (Fire Station)
- Health Centre
- School
- Neptune PH
- Fishermans Joy PH
- The Manhood School

A **B** **C** **D**

Nurseries

Street End

Fletchers

Nurseries

Lockgate

1

Chalder Farm

Mapsons Farm

Nurseries

CHALDER LANE

2

Highleigh Farm

Nurseries

Church Farm

3

Highleigh

Fletchers Estate

Nurseries

Haise Farm

Sidlesham

Littleton Barn

CRITCHELS LANE

Willow Glen

New Barn

4

Nurseries

Playing Field

Rookery Farm

Sch

Brent Lodge Bird & Wildlife Hospital

Keynor Copse

MANHOOD LA

5

Nurseries

Nurseries

Keynor Estate

OLDHOUSE LANE

Sheepwash Cottage

Nurseries

Nurseries

6

Keynor Rife

Bakers Farm

A **B** **C** **D**

The Index includes some names for which there is insufficient space on the maps. These names are indicated by an * and are followed by the nearest adjoining thoroughfare.

Old Market Av PO19 3 B5
Old Park La PO18 4 D6
Old Pl PO21 17 F2
Old Point PO22 21 E5
Old Rectory Ct PO22 20 A6
Old Rectory Dr PO20 12 B3
Old Rectory Gdns PO22 20 A6
Old School Cl PO20 23 E5
Old School Mews PO22 20 A5
Old School Pl PO20 12 A4
Oldhouse La PO20 27 A5
Oldlands Way PO22 19 G1
Oldwick Mdws PO18 8 B2
Oliver Whitby Rd PO19 6 A2
Olivers Mdw PO20 12 A3
Olivia Ct PO21 18 D6
Olivier Ct PO21 18 C2
Orchard Av, Chichester PO19 3 A1
Orchard Av, Selsey PO20 26 C3
Orchard Cotts PO18 5 G1
Orchard Cres BN18 11 A4
Orchard Gdns, Chichester PO19 3 A2
Orchard Gdns, Westergate PO20 12 A5
Orchard La PO20 22 A2
Orchard Par PO20 26 E2
Orchard Side PO20 9 A3
Orchard St PO19 3 A3
Orchard Way, Arundel BN18 11 A3
Orchard Way, Barnham PO22 13 E4
Orchard Way, Bognor Regis PO22 19 E3
Oriel Cl PO22 13 E4
Ormesby Cres PO22 19 H3
Ormonde Av PO19 7 E4
Orpen Pl PO20 26 E2
Osborne Cres, Portfield PO19 7 G3
Osborne Cres, Summersdale PO19 8 B6
Osprey Gdns PO22 19 E2
Otard Cl PO20 26 C3
Otter Cl PO19 6 B1
Otway Rd PO19 8 B5
Outerwyke Av PO22 20 A4
Outerwyke Gdns PO22 20 A4
Outerwyke Rd PO22 20 A4
Outram Rd PO22 19 H5
Outram Way PO20 9 B2
Oval La PO20 26 D4
Overdown Rd PO22 20 A5
Oving Rd PO19 7 E3
Oving Ter PO19 7 F3
Owers Way PO20 24 D4
Oxford Cl PO20 25 E3
Oxford Dr PO21 18 B5
Oxford St PO21 18 D6

Pacific Way PO20 26 D4
Paddock La PO20 26 B2
Paddocks PO22 13 E4
Pagham Rd, Bognor Regis PO21 16 B5
Pagham Rd, Chichester PO20 9 C2
Palace Yd PO19 3 B4
Palmer Pl PO20 9 D2
Palmers Field Av PO19 7 E1
Parchment St PO19 3 A1
Park Av PO20 26 E2
Park Cres PO20 26 F1
Park Dr, Arundel BN18 14 D4
Park Dr, Bognor Regis PO22 20 D5
Park La, Arundel BN18 11 B3
Park La, Chichester PO20 26 E1
Park Rd, Arundel BN18 14 D4
Park Rd, Barnham PO22 13 G4
Park Rd, Bognor Regis PO21 18 D6
Park Rd, Chichester PO20 26 F1
Park Ter PO21 18 D6
Park Walk PO19 3 D3
Parkers Cotts PO18 8 C1
Parkfield Av PO21 17 F2
Parklands Av PO21 19 E5
Parklands Rd PO19 3 A2
Parkway PO21 18 C5
Parsons Walk BN18 13 G2
Pasture Pl PO22 19 E3
Payne Cl PO21 16 C4
Peachey Rd PO20 26 C3
Peacock Cl PO19 8 D6
Pebble Cotts PO21 16 C3
Pebble Ct*, Macklin Rd PO22 19 G4
Peckhams Copse La PO20 7 G6
Peerley Cl PO20 25 F5
Peerley Rd PO20 25 F5
Pembroke Way PO21 18 A5
Penn Cl PO22 21 E5
Pennycord Cl PO20 26 D4
Pennyfields PO22 20 C4
Penwarden Way PO18 4 B2
Pescotts Cl PO20 23 F4
Peter Weston Pl PO19 3 D4
Peterhouse Cl PO21 18 B5
Pevensey Rd PO21 18 C4
Phillips Bsns Centre PO19 6 B4
Phoenix Cl PO19 3 D6
Piggery Hall La PO20 25 E2
Pilgrims Way PO21 16 D3
Pine Walk PO21 17 F1
Pinehurst Pk PO21 17 F1
Pinewood Gdns PO21 18 C5
Pinks La PO20 23 E6
Pipers Mead PO20 22 D6
Place St Maur Des Fosses PO21 19 F6
Plainwood Cl PO19 8 A5
Plover Cl, Bognor Regis PO22 19 E1
Plover Cl, Chichester PO20 25 F5
Pond Rd PO20 25 G6
Pook La PO18 8 B2
Portfield Retail Pk PO19 7 F2
Portfield Way PO19 7 F1
Post Office La PO20 9 D2
Poulner Cl PO22 20 A5
Pound Farm Rd PO19 7 E3
Pound Rd, Arundel BN18 13 G1
Pound Rd, Chichester PO20 24 A2
Poyntz Cl PO19 6 C6
Prawn Cl PO20 26 A1
Priestley Way PO22 20 D4
Prime Cl BN18 13 H2
Prince William Ct*, Lyon St PO21 19 F5
Princes Cft PO21 16 C4
Princess Av PO21 18 D6
Prior Pl PO19 7 E1
Priors Acre PO18 10 B2
Priors Waye PO21 16 C3
Priory Cl, Bognor Regis PO21 16 D4
Priory Cl, Chichester PO18 10 B2
Priory Ct*, Campbell Rd PO21 19 F5
Priory La PO19 3 C2
Priory Rd PO19 3 C2
Promenade PO21 19 E6
Pryors Grn PO21 17 E3
Pryors La PO21 16 D3
Pulborough Way PO22 20 D4
Pyrford Cl PO21 16 D3

Quarry La PO19 7 E4
Quarry La Ind Est PO19 7 F4
Queen Fields Walk PO21 18 B4
Queen Sq PO21 19 F5
Queens Av PO19 6 C5
Queens Fields Walk PO21 17 G1
Queens Flds East PO21 18 B4
Queens Flds West PO21 18 B4
Queens Gdns PO19 6 C5
Queensmead PO21 16 B5
Queensway, Aldwick PO21 17 F4
Queensway, Bognor Regis PO21 19 E5
Quest Cl PO19 7 E3

Radford Rd PO21 19 E3
Raleigh Rd PO21 16 D2
Ramillies Gdns PO22 20 C5
Ranworth Cl PO22 19 H3
Ratham La PO18 4 B2
Raughmere Copse PO18 8 B2
Raughmere Ct PO18 8 B3
Raughmere Dr PO18 8 B3
Ravens Way PO22 19 E2
Ravenwood Ct*, Aldwick St PO21 18 A6
Raycroft Cl PO21 17 H3
Red Ridges*, Kings Par PO21 18 C6
Redlands La PO20 22 A6
Redwood Pl PO21 17 G3
Regents Way PO21 18 B4
Regis Av PO21 16 D4
Regis Ct PO21 19 F5
Regnum Cotts PO19 8 C6
Regnum Ct PO19 3 B2
Renoir Ct PO22 18 D2
Renoir Mews PO22 18 C2
Rew La PO19 8 B4
Reynolds La BN18 11 D2
Richmond Av, Bognor Regis PO21 18 D6
Richmond Av, Chichester PO19 8 B6
Richmond Av West PO21 18 C6
Richmond Rd PO21 19 E5
Richmond Rd North PO21 19 F4
Richmond Villas*, Sea Rd PO22 19 H5
Rife La PO20 26 A1
Rife Way PO22 19 H4
Ripon Gdns PO21 18 A5
Riverside PO19 7 E3
Robins Cl PO20 26 C2
Robins Dr PO21 17 F1
Roche Ct PO19 6 C2
Rochester Cl PO19 8 B6
Rochester Way PO21 17 F2
Rock Gdns PO21 19 E6
Rockall Way PO18 4 C2
Rodney Cl PO21 17 E2
Rodney Cres BN18 15 G3
Rollaston Pk BN18 15 E4
Roman Flds PO21 18 C4
Roman Landing PO20 24 A1
Roman Way PO19 5 G3
Romney Broad Walk PO22 18 D2
Romney Garth PO20 26 D2
Rookery La PO20 27 D4
Rookwood Rd PO20 24 B1
Rose Av PO22 21 F5
Rose Cotts PO22 13 E5
Rose Ct PO21 17 E2
Rose Green Rd PO21 16 D2
Rosemary Cl PO21 17 E2
Ross Cl PO21 16 D3
Rossalyn Ct PO21 16 D2
Rostock Ct PO20 25 F5
Rosvara Av PO20 12 A3
Rotten Row PO20 27 A2
Round Piece PO20 26 A1
Roundle Av PO22 20 B4
Roundle Rd PO22 20 B4
Roundle Sq PO22 20 B4
Roundle Square Rd PO22 20 B4
Roundpiece La PO20 26 A2
Roundstone Way PO20 26 E1
Rowan Way PO22 18 D2
Royal Cl PO19 7 F3
Royal Par PO21 18 C3
Royce Cl PO20 24 B1
Royce Way PO20 24 B2
Rucrofts Cl PO21 17 H2
Rudford Ind Est BN18 15 G4
Rudwicks Cl PO22 20 C5
Rudwicks Way PO22 20 C6
Ruislip Gdns PO21 16 D3
Rumbolds Cl PO19 7 E4
Runcton La PO20 9 F2
Runnymede Ct PO21 18 B4
Rusbridge Cl PO21 17 F1
Ruskin Cl PO20 26 E3
Russell Pl*, High St PO21 19 F6
Russell Rd PO20 24 D4
Russell St PO19 7 E3
Rutland Way PO19 7 G1

Saddle La PO20 26 C2
Sadler St PO21 19 E6
Sadlers Walk PO19 3 C3
St Agnes Pl PO19 7 E3
St Andrews La PO20 10 A4
St Annes Ct PO20 25 E4
St Anthonys Walk PO21 17 E2
St Bartholomews Cl PO19 6 B3
St Blaises Rd PO18 10 A1
St Christophers Cl PO19 5 H3
St Claires Ter PO21 19 E5
St Clares Gdns PO21 18 C2
St Clares Mews PO22 19 H4
St Cyriacs PO19 3 B2
St Georges Cl PO20 26 D1
St Georges Dr PO19 6 C6
St Georges Walk PO20 12 B3
St Hildas Cl PO20 26 C3
St Itha Cl PO20 26 C3
St Itha Rd PO20 26 C3
St James Cl PO20 23 E4
St James Ind Est PO19 7 F2
St James Rd PO19 7 F2
St James Sq PO19 7 F2
St Johns Cl, Bognor Regis PO21 18 B4
St Johns Cl, Chichester PO20 12 A5
St Johns St PO19 3 C4
St Leodegars Way PO20 9 A2
St Martins Sq PO19 3 C3
St Martins St PO19 3 C3
St Marys Cl PO22 19 F3
St Marys Gdn PO19 3 C3
St Marys Mdw BN18 14 C3
St Marys Mews PO22 19 H4
St Marys Rd PO18 10 A2
St Nicholas Ct PO22 21 E4
St Nicholas La PO22 21 F5
St Nicholas Rd PO18 8 A1
St Pancras PO19 3 D3
St Pancras Ct*, St Pancras PO19 7 E3
St Pauls Gdns PO19 3 B1
St Pauls Rd PO19 3 A1
St Peters PO19 3 C2
St Peters Cl PO21 18 A5
St Peters Cres PO20 26 C1
St Richards Dr PO21 17 F1
St Richards Rd PO20 12 A3
St Richards Walk PO19 3 B4
St Richards Way PO21 17 F2
St Thomas Ct*, St Thomas Dr PO21 16 B5
St Thomas Dr PO21 16 B5
St Wilfreds Cl PO20 26 E1
St Wilfreds Vw PO20 26 A3
St Wilfrid Rd PO19 6 A2
St Winifreds Cl PO21 19 E6
Salisbury Way PO19 8 B6
Saltham La PO20 9 F2
Salthill La PO19 6 A1
Salthill Pk PO19 5 G1
Salthill Rd PO19 5 G3
Sandpiper Ct PO20 25 F5
Sandringham Cl PO20 25 G6
Sandringham Rd PO19 7 F3
Sandringham Way PO21 18 D4
Sandy Rd PO21 16 C5
Sandymount Av PO22 18 D3
Sandymount Cl PO22 19 E3
Sarisbury Cl PO22 20 A5
Satinwood Cl PO22 20 D4
Saxby Cl PO22 13 E5
Saxby Ct PO22 13 E5
Saxon Cl PO21 16 B5
Scholars Row PO22 13 F5
School Hill BN18 11 D2
School La, Bosham PO18 4 C4
School La, North Mundham PO20 9 D2
School La, Selsey PO20 26 C2
School La, Westergate PO20 12 B3
Scott Cl PO21 19 E6
Scott St PO21 19 E6
Sea Cl PO22 21 E5
Sea Dr PO22 20 C6
Sea Gro PO20 26 B3
Sea La, Middleton-on-Sea PO22 21 E5
Sea La, Pagham PO21 16 B5
Sea Rd PO22 19 H5
Sea Way, Elmer PO22 21 H5
Sea Way, Middleton-on-Sea PO22 20 D6
Sea Way, Pagham PO21 16 B5
Seabrook Cl PO21 17 F2
Seacourt Cl PO21 17 F3
Seafield Cl PO20 25 E5
Seafield Ter*, Marine Dr West PO21 17 H3
Seafield Way PO20 25 F5
Seagate Ct PO20 24 D5
Seagull Cl PO20 26 A1
Seal Rd PO20 26 B4
Seal Sq PO20 26 C4
Seaview Ct PO20 26 B4
Seaward Ct*, Chapel St PO21 19 E6
Seaward Dr PO20 24 B2
Second Av, Bognor Regis PO22 20 B6
Second Av, Chichester PO20 25 G6
Sedden Cl PO19 7 F1
Sefter Rd PO21 16 C1
Sefton Av PO21 17 F2
Selham Cl PO19 8 C4
Selsey Av PO21 18 C6
Selsey Rd, Chichester PO19 6 B6
Selsey Rd, Hunston PO20 7 E6
Selsey Rd, Sidlesham PO20 27 C2
Selwyn Cl PO21 18 B4
Senator Gdns PO19 5 G2
Servite Cl PO21 18 D4
Seymour Pl PO21 19 E5
Shalbourne Cres PO20 25 G6
Shamrock Cl, Bosham PO18 4 B4
Shamrock Cl, Chichester PO19 7 E1
Shaw Cl PO22 21 F5
Shearwater Dr PO22 19 E2
Sheepwash La, East Lavant PO18 8 B2
Sheepwash La, West Wittering PO20 22 A5
Shellbridge Rd BN18 11 E2
Shelley Rd PO21 18 D6
Sherborne Rd PO19 6 B3
Sherbourne La PO20 26 A1
Sherlock Av PO19 6 B2
Sherwood Cl PO22 18 D2
Sherwood Rd PO22 18 D3
Shingle Walk PO20 25 E5
Shipfield PO21 17 G3
Shipton Green La PO20 22 B5
Shirley Cl PO21 16 C5
Shirley Dr PO22 20 A4
Shirley Gdns PO22 20 A4
Shop La PO18 8 C2
Shopwhyke Ind Centre PO20 7 G2
Shopwhyke Rd PO20 7 G3
Shore Rd, Bosham PO18 4 A5
Shore Rd, East Wittering PO20 24 D5
Shorecroft PO21 17 G3
Shoreside Walk PO20 25 E4
Shripney La PO22 18 D1
Shripney Rd PO22 19 G1
Shrubbs Dr PO22 21 E5
Sidlesham La PO20 23 G4
Silver Birch Dr PO22 21 E4
Silver Way PO20 25 H6
Silverdale Cl PO21 16 C5
Silverlock Cl PO19 7 F2
Silverston Av PO21 18 C6
Simon Ct*, Crescent Rd PO21 19 E5
Singleton Cl PO21 16 D4
Slattsfield Cl PO20 26 D2
Slindon Bottom Rd BN18 11 A3
Sloe Cl PO19 7 F2
Smugglers La PO18 22 C1
Solent Rd PO20 25 E4
Solent Way PO20 26 C4
Somerset Gdns PO21 19 E3
Somerstown PO19 3 B1
Somerton Grn PO22 19 H3
South Av PO21 17 G2
South Bank PO19 6 C5
South Bersted Ind Est PO22 19 F2
South Dr PO22 20 C5
South Pallant PO19 3 C5
South Rd PO22 19 H3
South St PO19 3 B5
South Ter*, Shripney Rd PO22 19 F3
South Walk PO22 20 D5
South Way PO21 18 C3
Southcote Av PO20 24 D4
Southdean Cl PO22 21 F5
Southdean Dr PO22 21 E5
Southdown Cl PO19 7 F1
Southdown Ct PO20 25 F4
Southdown Rd PO21 19 E6
Southern Cross Ind Est PO22 19 G2
Southern Gate PO19 3 A6
Southern Rd PO20 26 C4
Southfield Ind Pk PO18 4 B3
Southfields Cl PO19 6 C6
Southgate PO19 3 B5
Southover Rd PO21 19 E5
Southview Rd PO22 20 B6
Southwark Walk PO21 17 F1
Sovereign Ct*, Campbell Rd PO21 19 F5
Sparshott Rd PO20 26 D4
Spencer St PO21 19 F5
Spinney Cl PO20 26 B1
Spinney La PO20 22 B3
Spinney Walk PO22 13 E4
Spitalfield La PO19 3 D1
Spitfire Ct PO20 10 B3
Springbank PO19 8 B6
Springfield PO21 16 C3
Springfield Cl, Birdham PO20 23 F4
Springfield Cl, Lavant PO18 8 A1
Sproule Cl BN18 15 E4
Spur Rd PO19 7 F4
Stable Fld PO22 21 G5
Stalham Way PO22 20 A4
Stanbrok Cl PO21 18 B5
Stanbury Cl PO18 4 B2
Stane St, Chichester PO20 7 G1
Stane St, Westhampnett PO18 10 A2
Stanford Cl PO22 19 G3
Stanley Cl PO21 19 F4
Stanmore Gdns PO21 17 G3
Stanover La PO22 20 A3
Stanton Dr PO19 8 B4
Staple La PO18 8 B1
Stapleton Ct PO21 17 F2
Station Rd, Arundel BN18 15 H1
Station Rd, Bognor Regis PO21 19 E5
Station Rd, Chichester PO18 4 B2
Stavely Gdns PO19 8 B4
Stempswood Way PO22 13 E4
Stephens Cl PO19 7 E2
Steyne St PO21 19 E6
Steyning Way PO22 19 G1
Stirling Rd PO19 3 D5
Stirling Way PO21 17 F3
Stockbridge Gdns PO19 6 B6
Stockbridge Rd PO19 3 B6
Stocker Rd PO21 18 D6
Stocks La, East Lavant PO18 8 C3
Stocks La, East Wittering PO20 25 E4
Stoneage Cl PO22 19 E1
Stonehill Cres PO21 16 D2
Stoney Stile Cl PO21 17 E3
Stoney Stile La PO21 17 E3
Storrington Cl PO19 5 G2
Story Rd PO19 7 F2
Strand Way PO22 20 B6
Strange Gdn PO21 17 G3
Stratton Ct PO22 19 G3
Stream Cl PO18 4 A4
Streathleigh Ct*, Kings Par PO21 18 C6

Street End La PO20 27 C2
Street End Rd PO20 27 C1
Streete Ct PO21 18 D6
Stride Cl PO19 7 F3
Stroud Green Dr PO21 18 B3
Stubcroft La PO20 25 F5
Stumps End PO18 4 B5
Stumps La PO18 4 B5
Sturges Rd PO21 19 E5
Sudbury Cl PO21 17 E3
Sudley Gdns PO21 19 F5
Sudley Rd PO21 19 F5
Summer La PO21 16 B3
Summerfield Rd PO20 24 B1
Summerhill Cl PO22 20 C4
Summerhill Dr PO22 20 C4
Summerley La PO22 20 B5
Summersdale Ct PO19 8 B4
Summersdale Rd PO19 8 C5
Sun Ct PO19 3 C5
Sun Park Cl PO21 18 C2
Sundale La PO22 21 E4
Sunderland Cl PO20 10 B3
Sunningdale Gdns, Bognor Regis PO22 18 D1
Sunningdale Gdns, Chichester PO20 24 C4
Sunny Way PO18 4 A4
Sunnybox La BN18 11 E3
Sunnymead Cl, Bognor Regis PO22 21 G4
Sunnymead Cl, Chichester PO20 26 D3
Sunnymead Dr PO20 26 D3
Sussex Ct PO22 21 G5
Sussex Dr PO21 16 C4
Sussex Gro PO20 25 G6
Sussex St PO21 19 F6
Sussex Village PO22 21 G5
Sutherland Cl PO21 19 E6
Sutton Cl PO22 19 H2
Swan Dene PO21 16 B5
Swanfield Dr PO19 7 E2
Swansea Gdns PO21 19 E6
Sycamore Rd PO22 19 E2
Sykes Cluan Cl PO22 12 D4
Sylvan Way PO21 18 D6
Sylvia Cl PO21 16 C3

Tabard Gate PO21 16 D3
Tack Lee Rd BN18 14 C3
Tamar Way PO20 10 B4
Tamarisk Cl PO22 19 E2
Tamarisk Walk PO20 24 D5
Tangmere Gdns PO21 17 E3
Tangmere Rd PO20 10 A3
Tannery Cl PO19 6 B3
Taverner Pl PO19 7 E5
Taylors La PO18 4 B6
Temlpesheen Rd PO22 21 G5
Templars Cl PO22 20 D4
Tenacre Cl PO19 7 E1
Tennyson Rd PO21 18 D5
Terminus Rd PO19 3 A6
Terminus Rd Ind Est PO19 3 A6
The Acorns PO21 18 C5
The Arcade PO21 19 F6
The Avenue, Bognor Regis PO21 18 D5
The Avenue, Chichester PO19 8 B5
The Bridgeway PO20 26 B3
The Bridle Way PO20 26 C3
The Broadway PO19 8 B5
The Bye Way PO21 17 E4
The Byeway PO20 24 B2
The Byway PO22 20 D5
The Causeway, Birdham PO20 23 F3
The Causeway, Bognor Regis PO21 16 C5
The Causeway, Selsey PO20 26 A2
The Chestnuts PO20 9 A3
The Clevets PO21 17 E3
The Close, Aldwick PO21 17 E4
The Close, Boxgrove PO18 10 B2
The Close, Chichester PO19 3 B4
The Close, Elmer PO22 21 G5
The Close, Lavant PO18 8 B2
The Close, Selsey PO20 26 E2
The Copse PO19 8 C5
The Cornfields PO20 12 A3
The Court PO21 16 C4
The Crescent, Chichester PO20 24 D4
The Crescent, Felpham PO22 20 A5
The Crescent, Pagham PO21 16 C4
The Croft, Arundel BN18 14 C3
The Croft, Bognor Regis PO21 18 C3
The Dell PO22 18 D2
The Drive, Arundel BN18 13 E1
The Drive, Bognor Regis PO21 17 E3
The Drive, Bosham PO18 4 B5
The Drive, Chichester PO19 8 B4
The Dunes PO21 16 D4
The Esplanade, Bognor Regis PO21 19 E6
The Esplanade, Felpham PO22 19 H5
The Fairway PO21 16 D5
The Glade PO21 16 C5
The Glebe PO20 10 A4
The Green, Bognor Regis PO21 16 C4
The Green, Chichester PO19 7 E2
The Grove PO22 20 A6
The Hard PO22 21 H5
The Hartings PO22 20 C3
The Heritage PO19 7 E3
The Hermitage PO20 9 D2
The Holdens PO18 4 A4
The Hollies PO21 18 B3
The Hopgarten PO21 18 B6
The Hornet PO19 3 D4
The Horseshoe PO20 26 B2
The Landerry Ind Est PO20 26 C2
The Lane PO19 8 B5
The Lawn PO21 17 G3
The Layne PO22 21 G5
The Limes BN18 14 C3
The Loop PO22 20 C6
The Lychgates BN18 14 C2
The Maltings PO19 3 A3
The Maples*, Hambledon Pl PO21 18 D5
The Meadows BN18 13 G2
The Mews*, Merchant St PO21 19 E5
The Midway PO22 20 A6
The Millers BN18 14 C4
The Nurseries PO21 17 E2
The Nyetimbers PO21 16 C3
The Oaks PO21 18 A5
The Old Stables PO22 19 H4
The Orchard PO21 17 E4
The Orchard Cl PO21 18 D5
The Paddock PO22 19 E3
The Parade PO21 16 C5
The Peacheries PO19 7 F4
The Pines BN18 14 C3
The Pitcroft PO19 7 F1
The Poplars BN18 14 C3
The Pound PO21 17 G2
The Precinct PO21 18 B5
The Providence PO19 3 B3
The Ridgeway PO22 20 A6
The Ridings, Arundel BN18 11 A4
The Ridings, Bognor Regis PO21 17 E4
The Rookery PO20 26 D2
The Saltings PO20 23 E5
The Spinney, Bognor Regis PO21 18 A5
The Spinney, Chichester PO20 22 A4
The Square PO22 13 E5
The Street, Arundel BN18 13 F1
The Street, Boxgrove PO18 10 B2
The Street, Itchenor PO20 22 A2
The Sussex Bsns Village PO22 13 G4
The Sycamores PO19 3 D1
The Thicketts PO21 17 E1
The View PO21 16 C5
The Wad PO20 24 A2
The Wadeway PO20 26 A2
The Waterplat PO19 7 E1
The Willows, Arundel BN18 15 H1
The Willows, Chichester PO20 26 D1
The Willows*, Victoria Dr PO21 18 D6
The Woodruff Bsns Centre PO19 6 B4
The Woolstaplers PO19 3 B3
Theatre La PO19 3 B4
Theatre Pl PO19 3 B4
Third Av, Bognor Regis PO22 20 B6
Third Av, Chichester PO20 25 G6
Thirlmere Way PO22 20 B4
Thompson Rd PO22 21 F5
Thorndene Av PO21 18 D4
Thorney Dr PO20 26 A3
Thrusloes PO21 17 H2
Tile Barn La PO20 25 H2
Tilford Dr PO22 19 G2
Timberlaine Ind Est PO19 7 E4
Tinghall PO21 17 G2
Tinwood La PO18 10 C1
Tithe Barn Cl PO21 16 D4
Tithe Barn Ct*, Tithe Barn Way PO21 16 D4
Tithe Barn Way PO21 16 D4
Tollhouse Cl PO19 3 A4
Tom Siggs Pl PO19 7 F4
Top Rd BN18 11 C1
Tower Cl PO19 3 B2
Tower Pl PO20 25 E4
Tower St PO19 3 B2
Town Cross Av PO21 19 E4
Tozer Way PO19 7 E3
Trafalgar Ct*, Norfolk Cl PO21 19 E6
Tramway Cl PO20 9 A3
Tregarth Rd PO19 8 C5
Trendle Grn PO21 18 B6
Tretawn Gdns PO20 26 E3
Trinity Way PO21 18 B5
Triton Pl PO22 20 B5
Trotyn Cft PO21 17 G2
Trundle Cl PO18 8 A1
Trundle View Cl PO22 13 E4
Truro Cl PO19 8 B6
Truro Cres PO21 17 G1
Tryndel Way PO22 20 B5
Tudor Cl, Bognor Regis PO22 20 D5
Tudor Cl, Chichester PO19 8 B5
Tudor Dr PO20 12 A2
Turnbull Rd PO19 3 D2
Turner Way PO20 26 E2
Turnpike Cl PO19 6 B6
Tuscan Av PO22 21 F5
Tye La BN18 13 G1
Tyne Way PO21 17 F1
Tythe Barn Rd PO20 26 C4

Ullswater Gro PO22 20 B4
Uphill Way PO20 9 A3
Uppark Way PO22 20 C3
Upper Bognor Rd PO21 19 F4
Upton Rd PO19 6 C5
Ursula Av PO20 26 C4
Ursula Av North PO20 26 C3
Ursula Sq PO20 26 C4

Valentines Gdns PO21 17 E3
Van Dyck Pl PO22 18 D2
Van Gogh Pl PO22 18 D2
Velyn Av PO19 7 E3
Venus La PO21 16 A6
Verica Ct PO19 5 G2
Via Ravenna PO19 3 A5
Vicarage La PO22 19 H4
Vicars Cl PO19 3 B4
Victoria Ct*, Aldwick Rd PO21 18 C6
Victoria Dr PO21 18 D6
Victoria Gdns PO20 12 A3
Victoria Rd, Bognor Regis PO21 18 D6
Victoria Rd, Chichester PO19 7 F3
Victoria Rd South PO21 18 D6
Victoria Ter*, Sea Rd PO22 19 H5
Victory Ct*, Norfolk Cl PO21 19 E6
Villa Plage PO22 21 G5
Vincent Rd PO20 26 B3
Vinnetrow Rd PO20 7 G4
Viscount Dr PO21 16 D5

Wade End PO20 26 A2
Wadhurst Cl PO21 18 D4
Wakefield Way PO21 17 F1
Walberton Cl PO22 20 A4
Wallfield PO21 17 G3
Wallner Cres PO22 20 C5
Walmsleys Way PO20 25 H6
Walnut Av PO19 3 A1
Walsham Cl PO22 19 H3
Walton Av PO21 19 G6
Walton La PO18 4 B4
Walton Rd PO21 19 F6
Walwyn Cl PO20 23 F5
Wandleys Cl PO20 12 C1
Wandleys Dr PO20 12 C1
Wandleys La, Arundel BN18 11 A4
Wandleys La, Chichester PO20 12 C1
Wansford Way PO22 20 B6
Warbleheath Cl PO18 8 B1
Warblers Way PO22 18 D1
Waremere Ct BN18 14 D3
Warner Rd PO20 26 B3
Warners La PO20 26 A1
Warren Farm La PO19 8 B5
Warren Way PO22 13 E5
Warwick Cl PO21 16 C3
Warwick Pl PO22 20 D5
Washington St PO19 3 B1
Waterloo Rd PO22 19 H4
Waterloo Sq PO21 19 E6
Waterloo Sq Gdns PO21 19 E6
Waters Edge PO21 17 G3
Waterside Dr PO19 6 C6
Waterside Gdns PO20 24 D4
Watersmeet PO19 5 H3
Waterstone Cl PO20 22 A2
Watery La PO19 6 D6
Watson Way PO20 12 A3
Waverley Rd PO21 18 D4
Webb Cl PO21 16 C5
Wedgwood Rd PO22 20 A6
Well Rd PO21 16 B6
Wellington Gdns PO20 26 C1
Wellington Rd, Bognor Regis PO21 19 E6
Wellington Rd, Chichester PO19 8 B6
Wells Cres, Bognor Regis PO21 18 A5
Wells Cres, Chichester PO19 8 A6
Wellsfield PO20 24 B2
Wentworth Cl PO22 13 E4
Wessex Av, Bognor Regis PO21 18 D6
Wessex Av, Chichester PO20 25 F4
West Av, Aldwick PO21 18 B6
West Av, Middleton-on-Sea PO22 21 E4
West Bank BN18 14 D1
West Beach PO20 24 C4
West Beach Rd PO20 24 C4
West Bracklesham Dr PO20 25 E5
West Cl, Felpham PO22 20 B6
West Cl, Middleton-on-Sea PO22 20 D5
West Dr, Aldwick PO21 16 D4
West Dr, Middleton-on-Sea PO22 21 F5
West Front Rd PO21 16 B6
West Meads Dr PO21 18 B3
West Pallant PO19 3 B4
West Sands La PO20 26 A2
West St, Bognor Regis PO21 19 E6
West St, Chichester PO19 3 A3
West St, Selsey PO20 26 A3
West Strand PO20 24 A3
West View Dr BN18 14 C4
West Vw PO19 5 G3
West Walberton La BN18 11 B4
Westbridge Path PO18 8 A3
Westbrook Cl PO18 4 A4
Westbrook Fld PO18 4 A4
Westergate Mews PO20 12 A3
Westergate St PO20 12 A5
Westerley Gdns*, Bracklesham La PO20 25 F6
Western Rd PO20 26 D3
Westfield PO22 18 D2
Westgate PO19 3 A3
Westhampnett By-Pass PO19 7 G2
Westhampnett Rd PO19 7 F2
Westingway PO21 18 C5
Westlands PO20 23 E3
Westlands La PO20 22 C4
Westlands Rd PO20 9 A3
Westloats Gdns PO21 18 D4
Westloats La PO21 18 D4
Westmead Rd PO19 5 H3
Westminster Dr PO21 17 F1
Westmorland Dr PO22 20 A4
Westward Cl PO18 4 B4
Westward Ho PO19 5 H3
Westway PO22 19 F4
Wheatfield Rd PO20 26 E1
Whistler Av PO19 8 B6
Whitebeam Way, Bognor Regis PO22 20 D4
Whitebeam Way, Chichester PO20 10 B4
Whitelands PO22 20 A4
Whiteside Cl PO19 7 E2
Whiteways PO22 18 C2
Whiteways Cl PO22 18 C2
Whitfield Cl PO22 19 G3
Whyke Cl PO19 7 E5
Whyke Ct PO19 7 E5
Whyke La PO19 3 D4
Whyke Rd PO19 7 E5
Wick Cl PO22 20 B5
Wick La PO22 20 B5
Widgeon La PO20 26 A1
Widworthy Mews*, Sylvan Way PO21 18 D6
Wight Way PO20 26 D4
William Cawley Mews PO19 3 B1
William Rd PO19 7 G3
William St PO21 19 F5
Williams Rd PO18 4 B2
Willow Brook PO22 21 F5
Willow Ct PO19 6 A3
Willow Way PO21 16 D4
Willowbed Av PO19 7 E5
Willowbed Dr PO19 7 E5
Willowhale Av PO21 17 F3
Willowhale Grn PO21 17 E3
Wills Cl BN18 15 E4
Wilman Gdns PO21 17 E2
Wilson Cl PO19 6 A2
Wilson Ct BN18 15 E4
Wilton Cl PO20 25 G6
Winchester Dr PO19 6 C1
Winden Av PO19 7 E3
Windmill Cl PO21 16 D3
Windmill Ct, East Wittering PO20 25 E4
Windmill Ct, Tangmere PO20 10 B4
Windmill Fld PO18 4 A4
Windsor Cl PO21 18 B4
Windsor Dr PO20 24 D4
Windsor Rd, Chichester PO19 7 F3
Windsor Rd, Selsey PO20 26 C3
Wingard Way PO19 3 C6
Winston Cl PO21 18 C2
Winston Cres PO21 18 B2
Winterbourne Rd PO19 8 C5
Wiston Av PO19 6 B5
Wolsey Cl PO21 16 D3
Wood St PO21 18 D6
Woodborough Cl PO20 25 G5
Woodend PO21 18 C5
Woodfield Cl, Bognor Regis PO21 16 C5
Woodfield Cl, Chichester PO20 10 B4
Woodgate Cl PO20 12 A5
Woodgate Pk PO20 12 A5
Woodgate Rd PO20 12 A5
Woodland Pl PO19 8 B4
Woodland Rd PO20 26 C4
Woodlands La PO19 6 C1
Woodlands Pk BN18 14 C3
Woodlands Rd PO22 18 D2
Woodside PO22 13 E4
Woodstock Gdns PO21 17 G3
Worcester Cl PO21 18 B5
Worcester Rd PO19 8 A6
Wordsworth Gdns PO22 20 D4
Worms La PO22 20 C3
Wren Cres PO22 18 D2
Wrenfield Pl*, Scott Cl PO21 19 E6
Wroxham Way PO22 19 H3
Wyatt Ct PO20 25 E4
Wychwood Cl PO21 17 F3
Wychwood Walk PO21 17 F3
Wyde Feld PO21 17 H3
Wyke La North PO22 20 B4
Wythering Cl PO21 16 B6
Wyvern Cl PO20 10 C4

Yapton La BN18 11 F4
Yapton Rd, Barnham PO22 13 E5
Yapton Rd, Horsemere Green BN17,18 15 E4
Yapton Rd, Middleton-on-Sea PO22 21 E4
Yeomans Acre PO21 18 B5
Yew Tree Cl PO22 18 D2
York Chase PO19 8 B6
York Rd, Bognor Regis PO21 19 F6
York Rd, Chichester PO19 7 E4
York Rd, Selsey PO20 26 C4
Young St PO19 8 C6